Acknowledgments

S0-BCJ-394

The authors would like to thank the Insulin BASICS Team at the International Diabetes Center, Minneapolis, for their commitment to the program and to our clients.

Peggy Baldy

Susan Beck, BSN, RN

Richard M. Bergenstal, MD

Nancy Cooper, RD, LD, CDE

Janet Davidson, BSN, RN, CDE

Tamara Eiden

Paula Ekerholm, MS, RD, LD, CDE

Deborah Elsen, BSN, RN, CDE

Colleen Fischer, RD, LD, CDE

David Kendall, MD

Julie Kunz, RD, LD, CDE

Amy Moore, MS, RN, CDE

Leah Olson, BSN, RN

Jan Pearson, BAN, RN, CDE

Diane Reader, RD, LD, CDE

Jennifer Robinett, BSN, RN, CDE

Joy Smetanka, RD, LD, CDE

Sue Sorensen, RD, LD, CDE

TABLE OF CONTENTS

Welcome

In this session you will:

- gain an understanding of diabetes and what causes it

- learn the reasons for insulin therapy and the goals of treatment

- discover or review the importance of controlling blood glucose levels

- learn or review how and when to test your blood glucose

- learn about the kinds of insulin and how they work

- learn how to measure and inject insulin

- begin to learn about carbohydrate foods and how to eat consistently

- learn the symptoms and treatment for hypoglycemia (low blood glucose)

- begin to feel better about your ability to manage diabetes

What Is Diabetes?

Diabetes is a condition that causes high blood glucose (blood sugar) levels. It is a chronic disease that can be managed but not cured. It doesn't go away.

Proper diabetes treatment and education can help you stay healthy. You can learn to live well with diabetes. That is our goal.

Without proper treatment, diabetes can cause damage to the large and small blood vessels. Blood vessel damage can lead to serious nerve, heart, eye, or kidney problems. But this doesn't have to happen.

You are taking an important step toward living well with diabetes by starting to take insulin. Many people will help you along the way. These include your doctor, nurse educators, registered dietitians, other health professionals, and your family and friends. They are all on your team.

Glucose and Insulin

Much of the food we eat is digested and changed into glucose. Glucose is the body's main energy source. It is carried in the bloodstream to the body's cells. Inside the cells, it is converted into energy.

Insulin helps glucose get into the cells. Insulin is a hormone made in the pancreas. It attaches to cells in the body. It opens the cells to allow glucose to get inside.

Diabetes is caused by a breakdown in this process. Insulin is either absent or poorly used, so glucose stays in the bloodstream. Glucose that stays in the bloodstream causes blood glucose levels to rise.

Insulin injections help to keep blood glucose levels from going or staying too high.

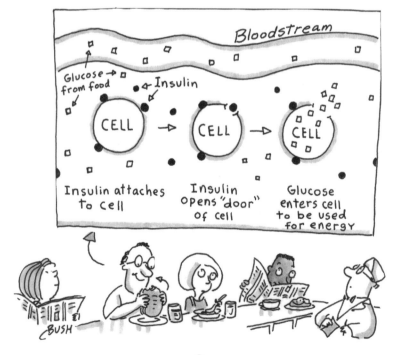

Types of Diabetes

There are three types of diabetes. Each type occurs for a different reason. All three types of diabetes cause high blood glucose levels.

TYPE 1 DIABETES

The immune system destroys the insulin-producing cells in the pancreas. The cells stop making insulin. This means that the body can't use glucose for energy. That's why people with type 1 diabetes need insulin injections every day to stay alive. Type 1 diabetes usually occurs in children or in young adults under age 30.

TYPE 2 DIABETES

The pancreas does not make enough insulin or the body cannot use insulin properly. The body "resists" the action of insulin. Glucose doesn't get into the body's cells very well. Treatment for type 2 diabetes includes a food plan and exercise. Sometimes diabetes pills or insulin injections are needed. Type 2 diabetes is more common in people over age 45, but even children can develop it.

GESTATIONAL DIABETES

In some women, the hormonal changes of pregnancy demand more insulin than the body can make. Sometimes, blood glucose levels can be controlled with a food plan and exercise. If not, then insulin injections or a diabetes pill may be needed during the pregnancy. After the birth of the baby, blood glucose levels usually return to normal. A woman who has had gestational diabetes is at risk for developing type 2 diabetes later in life.

Diagnosing Diabetes

Diabetes is diagnosed through blood tests that measure the glucose level in the blood. Two tests are used:

- A fasting blood glucose test is done when a person has had nothing but water for at least eight hours.

- A casual, or random, blood glucose test can be done at any time.

These tests show whether the blood glucose level is too high. If it is, you have diabetes.

Sometimes, however, blood glucose levels are higher than normal but not high enough to be diabetes. Two conditions cause this. They are impaired glucose tolerance and impaired fasting glucose. People with these conditions are at risk for diabetes.

DIAGNOSIS	FASTING TEST	CASUAL TEST
Diabetes	126 mg/dL or higher	200 mg/dL or higher and symptoms
Normal	Less than 110 mg/dL	140 mg/dL or lower

Symptoms of Diabetes

Diabetes has both "classic" and "common" symptoms. Both types are symptoms of high blood glucose, or hyperglycemia.

CLASSIC SYMPTOMS	COMMON SYMPTOMS
Frequent urination	Fatigue
Increased thirst	Blurred vision
Increased hunger	Frequent infections and poor wound healing
Unexplained weight loss	Numbness and tingling in hands, legs, and feet

Classic symptoms are usually linked with type 1 diabetes. Common symptoms occur more often with type 2 diabetes. Some people with type 2 diabetes also experience classic symptoms.

You may have many symptoms or none at all. And symptoms can clear up with treatment and then return when diabetes is not well controlled. You may feel the same symptoms as when you were first diagnosed.

Even if you never have symptoms, it's important to do everything you can to manage your diabetes. Start today!

Ketones

When the body lacks insulin and cannot use glucose for energy, it may start to burn fat. Fat is the body's second source of energy, after glucose.

Burning fat may seem like a good thing, but it can create a buildup of acids in the urine and blood called ketones. Ketones are a sign that your blood glucose level may be very high. This can cause a serious chemical imbalance in your body.

People with type 1 diabetes have the greatest risk for developing ketones. Some people with type 2 diabetes may also develop ketones.

You can use special strips to test your urine for ketones. The test tells you if your urine contains a small, moderate, or large amount of ketones or none at all. The higher the amount, the more serious it is.

In addition to urine strips, there are now meters that measure ketones from a small drop of blood. You get the blood from a finger stick.

You may have positive ketone tests when you first start to take insulin. This is normal, and it may continue for awhile. The amount will gradually decrease. Ketones may reappear if you don't eat for a period of time or if you don't take enough insulin.

Your provider will tell you if you need to test for ketones. You will learn how to do a ketone test and what the results mean.

Diabetes Treatment

The goals of diabetes treatment are to help you feel better and:

- keep blood glucose levels within a target range
- balance your insulin needs with your eating habits, activity level, and lifestyle
- prevent, delay, or slow the progression of health problems related to diabetes

Blood glucose control is your primary treatment goal. If blood glucose is very high over a long period of time, you can have other health problems. You can help prevent this from happening by following a diabetes treatment plan.

Treatment options are shown on page 9. A food and activity plan is the core of diabetes treatment. Diabetes pills and insulin are used as well.

Your treatment is based on what your body needs. If you have type 1 diabetes, you must take insulin to keep your blood glucose levels in control. If you have type 2 diabetes or gestational diabetes, and other treatments aren't working, you may need to take insulin.

Many people with type 2 diabetes take one or more diabetes pills to help control blood glucose levels. The table on pages 102–103 shows the diabetes pills now available.

If you have been taking diabetes pills, you may need to continue taking them along with insulin. Your provider may change the type of pill you take. Certain diabetes pills can help the body use insulin better.

DIABETES TREATMENT OPTIONS

Food & Activity Plan

Food & Activity Plan   +   Diabetes Pill

Food & Activity Plan   +   Diabetes Pill   +   Diabetes Pill

Food & Activity Plan   +   Diabetes Pill(s)   +   Insulin

Food & Activity Plan   +   Insulin

Blood Glucose Self-test

You may already be testing your blood glucose levels. Now that you're taking insulin, you need to continue testing. You may need to test more often than you have in the past.

If you are new to testing, you will learn how to do it using a blood glucose meter. The meter gives you an immediate reading of your blood glucose level at the moment you test.

You and your provider will work out a testing schedule to meet your needs. Regular testing is very important when taking insulin.

You also need to keep a record of your test results and insulin doses in your Diabetes Record Book. Regular testing and record keeping help you and your provider:

- evaluate your blood glucose control

- decide what insulin regimen or dose changes you may need to improve control

- see how food, activity, and insulin affect your blood glucose levels

- determine how well your treatment plan is working

| Date | 3 AM BG | BREAKFAST | | | LUNCH | | | DINNER | | | BEDTIME | |
		BG	Med	BG	BG	Med	BG	BG	Med	BG	BG	Med
6-5		220	8 R/ 16 NPH		291			192	6 R/ 6 NPH		320	
6-6		256	"		285			250	"		297	
6-7		201	"		266			211	"		301	

Self-test Times and Targets

When you begin taking insulin, you need to test your blood glucose level at certain times every day. The times for testing are:

- before breakfast

- before lunch

- before dinner

- before bedtime snack

- sometimes two hours after the start of meals

Each time you test your blood, you are aiming for a blood glucose level within a target range. The range is different depending on the time of your test. You can expect your blood glucose level to go up after meals. But you don't want it to go up too high.

TEST TIME	TARGET RANGE
Before meals	80–140 mg/dL
Two hours after start of meals:	
Taking Regular	Less than 180 mg/dL
Taking Lispro or Aspart	Within 20–40 mg/dL of pre-meal level
Bedtime	100–140 mg/dL

Sometimes your blood glucose level will be outside the target range. That's okay. Your blood glucose levels don't have to be perfect. Eventually, your goal is to have at least one-half of your readings (50%) in your target range.

Simple Steps for Self-testing

Follow this simple procedure to test your blood glucose level. You will need certain supplies for testing. Your provider can tell you what they are. (See page 104.)

1. Wash hands with soap and warm water. Dry thoroughly.

2. Put a test strip into the meter. (See meter instructions.)

3. Poke your finger with the lancing device.

4. Gently massage the area until a drop of blood forms.

5. Place the blood drop on the test strip.

6. Wait for the test result to be displayed.

7. Record the result in your Diabetes Record Book.

TESTING TIPS

- Shake your arm down to get more blood into your fingers.

- Press the lancing device tight against the side of your finger tips.

- Change the site each time you test. Use all ten fingers.

- Keep test strips covered, dry, and in packaging until used.

- Don't let test strips get below 36 degrees or above 90 degrees Fahrenheit.

- Follow instructions supplied by the meter manufacturer.

- Dispose of lancets properly. (See page 25.)

Hemoglobin A$_{1c}$ Test

During your regular visits, your provider will often draw a blood sample. The sample is used for another blood glucose test. It is called a Hemoglobin A$_{1c}$ test (HbA$_{1c}$). This test measures your average blood glucose level over the past two months. The value is reported as a percentage (%).

Ideally, you should have an HbA$_{1c}$ test every three to four months. The target for HbA$_{1c}$ is no more than 1 to 1.5 percentage points over normal.

When at least half of your self-tested blood glucose levels are within the target range, your HbA$_{1c}$ will usually be in target, too. Reaching your HbA$_{1c}$ target may take up to several months. Ask your provider to help you fill in the blanks below.

....

The normal range for my provider's lab is _____ to _____.
My target HbA$_{1c}$ is _____%.

Based on a normal of 6%, if your HbA$_{1c}$ is:	then your average blood glucose level is:
4%	60
5%	90
6%	120
7%	150
8%	180
9%	210
10%	240
11%	270
12%	300
13%	330

About Insulin

Insulin works together with glucose to provide energy. There are two main kinds of injected insulin.

- *Bolus insulin* supplies a burst of insulin. It's usually used before a meal. There are two kinds of bolus insulin: rapid-acting and short-acting. Rapid-acting insulin works quickly and then is gone from the body. Short-acting insulin stays in the body longer.

- *Background insulin* provides a low level of insulin throughout the day or overnight. There are three kinds of background insulin: intermediate-acting, prolonged intermediate-acting, and long-acting. Long-acting insulin lasts longer in the body than intermediate-acting insulin or prolonged intermediate-acting insulin.

Sometimes bolus insulin and background insulin come mixed together. This is called *premixed insulin*.

The table on the next page shows the different kinds of insulin now available. It also shows the timing for how each one works after it's injected.

The time when insulin is working hardest is called its "peak effect." After the peak effect, insulin gradually works less and less. After awhile it stops working effectively to lower blood glucose.

BOLUS INSULIN	BEGINS TO WORK	WORKING HARDEST	STOPS WORKING EFFECTIVELY
Rapid-acting			
Lispro (Humalog®)	5–15 minutes	30–75 minutes	2–4 hours
Aspart (Novolog®)	5-15 minutes	1–2 hours	3–6 hours
Short-acting			
Regular	30–45 minutes	2–3 hours	4–8 hours

BACKGROUND INSULIN	BEGINS TO WORK	WORKING HARDEST	STOPS WORKING EFFECTIVELY
Intermediate-acting			
NPH	2–4 hours	4–8 hours	10–16 hours
Lente	2–4 hours	4–8 hours	10–16 hours
Prolonged intermediate-acting			
Ultralente	3–5 hours	8–12 hours	18-20 hours
Long-acting			
Glargine (Lantus®)	4–8 hours	No peak	24 hours

PREMIXED INSULIN	BEGINS TO WORK	WORKING HARDEST	STOPS WORKING EFFECTIVELY
(bolus/background together)		**Early peak– Late peak**	
75/25	5–15 minutes	1–12 hours	about 18 hours
70/30 or 50/50	30–60 minutes	2–12 hours	about 18 hours

Your Insulin Plan

Your provider will recommend an insulin plan that works best for you. The plan is based on your individual needs, your eating habits, and your lifestyle.

Your insulin plan tells you:

- which insulin to take (you may take more than one kind)

- what dose of each kind of insulin to take

- when to take your insulin

An insulin plan is also known as an insulin regimen. There are many different regimens. The most common ones include two, three, or four injections a day.

There are different combinations of insulin injections. Usually injections are taken before some meals. You might take one at bedtime.

The exact timing of injections before meals depends on whether your bolus insulin is rapid-acting or short-acting.

Rapid-acting *Lispro insulin* (Humalog) and *Aspart insulin* (Novolog) start to work very quickly. They need to be taken immediately before beginning to eat. It's best to wait until the food is on the table.

Short-acting *Regular insulin* needs to be taken thirty to forty-five minutes before eating.

INSULIN TIPS

- Always take your insulin. Never skip a dose.

- Try to take your insulin at about the same times every day.

Most people take a combination of bolus insulin and background insulin. At times, the two are mixed together in a single syringe. They are then injected in the same shot. At other times just one kind of insulin is injected. The graphs below show two sample regimens.

THREE-INJECTION REGIMEN WITH SHORT-ACTING INSULIN
This regimen uses Regular insulin (bolus) and NPH insulin (background) in three injections. Notice how Regular insulin is present for breakfast and dinner. See how the morning NPH helps to cover lunch and works into the afternoon? The bedtime NPH works overnight.

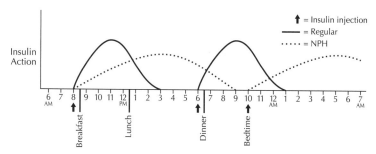

THREE-INJECTION REGIMEN WITH RAPID-ACTING INSULIN
This example shows Lispro insulin (bolus) and Ultralente insulin (background) in three injections. The Lispro covers each meal. The Ultralente provides a base of insulin through-out the day and overnight.

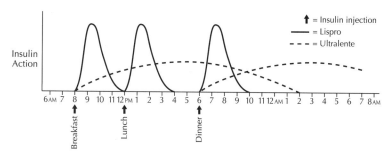

17

How to Measure Insulin

If you are just starting insulin, you might be nervous about taking your first injection. Most people find that it isn't as bad as they thought it would be.

In order to take insulin, you first need to learn how to draw it up into the syringe. You'll learn to draw up one kind of insulin by itself. You'll also learn to draw up two kinds of insulin to inject together.

You can mix bolus insulin and background insulin together in the same syringe. Bolus insulin is clear. Most background insulin is cloudy. This is a quick way to tell them apart when measuring them.

Glargine insulin (Lantus) is the only kind of background insulin that is not cloudy. It is clear. Glargine is never mixed with other kinds of insulin. It doesn't work right when it's mixed.

INSULIN TIPS

- Always wash your hands before you inject insulin.

- If you mix two kinds of insulin together, draw up the bolus insulin first.

- If you make a mistake, empty the syringe and start over.

- Never mix Glargine with another insulin in the same syringe.

Measuring One Kind of Insulin

1. Wash hands. Wipe bottle top with alcohol.

2. If the insulin is cloudy, roll bottle to mix.

3. Remove syringe cover.

4. Pull plunger to draw air into syringe equal to your insulin dose.

5. Put needle into insulin bottle. Push plunger to shoot air into the bottle.

6. Leave needle in bottle. Turn bottle and syringe upside down. Make sure needle tip is in the insulin.

7. Pull down on plunger and push up to remove air bubbles from syringe.

8. Pull plunger to measure your exact dose of insulin.

9. Remove needle from bottle.

10. Inject insulin.

Clear to cloudy

Measuring Two Kinds of Insulin

1. Wash hands. Wipe bottle tops with alcohol.
   N
2. Roll background (cloudy) insulin bottle.
3. Remove syringe cover.
   N
4. Pull plunger to draw air into syringe equal to your background insulin dose.
   N
5. Put needle into background insulin bottle. Push plunger to shoot air into the bottle.
6. Remove needle from the insulin bottle.
7. Pull plunger to draw air into syringe equal to your bolus *R* (clear) insulin dose. *R*
8. Put needle into bolus insulin bottle. Push plunger to shoot air into the bottle.
9. Leave needle in the insulin bottle. Turn bottle and syringe upside down. Make sure needle tip is in the insulin.
10. Pull down on plunger and push up to remove air bubbles from syringe.
11. Pull plunger to measure your bolus insulin dose.
12. Remove needle from bolus insulin bottle.
    N
13. Put needle into background insulin bottle. Turn bottle and syringe upside down.
14. Pull plunger to measure your *total* insulin dose. Your total dose is your bolus insulin dose plus your background insulin dose.
15. Remove needle from bottle.
16. Inject insulin.

NOTE: Never mix Glargine (Lantus) with another insulin in the same syringe. Glargine is a clear background insulin. It won't work properly if it is mixed with another insulin.

Insulin Injection Tips

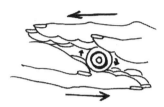

IF THE INSULIN YOU ARE MEASURING IS CLOUDY, ROLL IT
BETWEEN YOUR HANDS TO MIX IT BEFORE YOU DRAW IT UP.

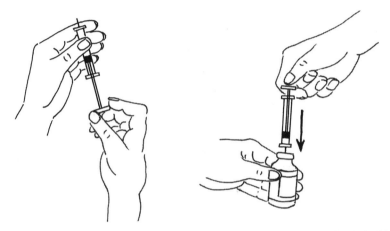

BEFORE YOU DRAW UP YOUR INSULIN DOSE, PULL THE SYRINGE PLUNGER DOWN
TO DRAW AIR INTO THE SYRINGE EQUAL TO YOUR DOSE. NEXT, INSERT THE
SYRINGE NEEDLE INTO THE TOP OF THE BOTTLE AND PUSH THE PLUNGER TO
SHOOT AIR INTO THE BOTTLE. THEN YOU ARE READY TO DRAW UP YOUR DOSE.

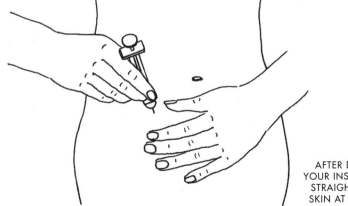

AFTER DRAWING UP
YOUR INSULIN, INJECT IT
STRAIGHT INTO YOUR
SKIN AT A 90° ANGLE.

How and Where to Inject Insulin

Insulin is injected into the fatty tissue just under your skin. The standard needle is only ½-inch long and very thin. Some people who are very lean may use a shorter needle (⁵⁄₁₆-inch). Ask your provider which kind is best for you.

To give an injection, place the needle at a 90-degree angle to your skin. Then push it straight in. It slips in very easily. People are often surprised at how painless injections are.

Be sure to push the syringe plunger in all the way. Then remove the needle. When using an insulin pen, count to five before removing the needle. These techniques ensure that you inject your full insulin dose.

After taking an injection, hold your finger over the injection site for a few seconds. This helps the insulin to be completely absorbed.

INSULIN TIPS

- Insert the needle into your skin at a 90-degree angle.

- Inject your insulin at least a thumb-width away from your last injection site.

- Avoid injecting insulin into surgical scars.

The abdomen is usually the best place to inject insulin. This area absorbs insulin quickly and efficiently. But you can also use other parts of your body. The illustration below shows where to give injections.

Try not to use exactly the same spot for every injection. For example, give one injection in the right side of your stomach area and the next in the left. Repeated injections in the same spot may cause skin to break down (atrophy). Or skin may become scarred or swollen (hypertrophy).

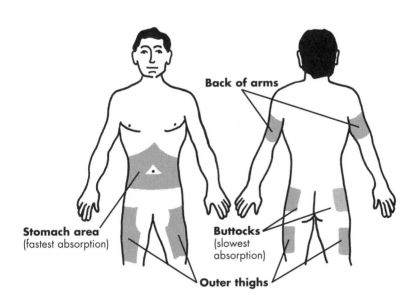

Back of arms

Stomach area
(fastest absorption)

Buttocks
(slowest absorption)

Outer thighs

Storing Your Insulin

Extreme temperatures can cause insulin to lose its effectiveness. Also, like most medications, insulin is clearly marked with an expiration date. After it expires, insulin will not work properly and should not be used.

Sometimes you can tell that insulin should not be used. And sometimes you can't. To be safe, never use insulin that:

- is past its expiration date

- sticks to the inside of the bottle, appears lumpy, or has changed color

- has been exposed to temperatures below 32 degrees or above 86 degrees Fahrenheit

To make sure your insulin doesn't go "bad," store unopened bottles, cartridges, and pens in the refrigerator. Opened bottles may be stored in the refrigerator or at room temperature. But keep opened pens and cartridges at room temperature. Do not refrigerate them.

Properly stored insulin remains effective until its expiration date. When opened, however, it must be used within a certain period of time or it loses its effectiveness. Bottles of open insulin are good for thirty days. Insulin pens and cartridges may be effective anywhere from seven to thirty days. Be sure to check the package insert to find out how long you can keep using your insulin after opening it.

"Sharps" Disposal

Syringe needles and lancets are called "sharps." They need to be disposed of properly to make sure others are not injured. Common methods of disposal include:

- a sharps container, available at some pharmacies. When full, return the container to the pharmacy for disposal.

- a safety clip, which cuts off the needle. When the unit is full, throw it in your regular garbage.

- a puncture-resistant container. Examples include a detergent bottle, a soft-drink bottle, or a coffee can. Label the container "sharps." When full, put the cap on and seal it securely with tape. Throw it in your regular garbage.

Contact your local sanitation agency to check which method they prefer. Some trash collection companies will not pick up sharps. Check with your pharmacy about disposal methods in your area.

INSULIN TIPS

- Always buy the same brand of insulin.

- Keep an extra bottle of each kind of insulin that you take in the refrigerator.

- Check the package insert to find out how long you can use open insulin.

- Be sure to dispose of "sharps" properly.

Your Diabetes Food Plan

A diabetes food plan is very important when you take insulin. Your provider needs to know what, when, and how much you like to eat. This helps to determine the right insulin plan for you.

You may already have a diabetes food plan. If so, your provider will work with you to develop an insulin plan that works with it. If you want to make changes to your food plan, be sure to let your provider know.

If you don't have a food plan, your dietitian will design one based on your eating habits. Next your provider determines your insulin plan based on your food plan.

My Eating Habits   **My Food Plan**   **My Insulin Plan**

You will be able to enjoy all the foods you like and still take care of your diabetes. You won't have to eat special foods or the same foods every day. There is no strict diabetes diet.

Your diabetes food plan can help you eat in a healthy manner and:

- keep your blood glucose levels in the target range

- maintain healthy cholesterol and triglyceride levels

- reach or maintain a healthy body weight

- prevent diabetes complications

Consistency Counts!

Over the next few weeks, you will work with your provider to determine your insulin plan. Eating consistently from day to day will help with this process.

You need to eat your meals at about the same times each day. It's usually okay to eat within one hour of your usual time. You may have snacks if you like.

You also need to eat about the same amounts of food at each meal. For example, eating one slice of bread is about the same as eating one small roll. Eating one apple is about the same as eating an orange. Drinking a cup of milk is about the same as eating a cup of yogurt.

Eating consistently also means eating every meal every day.

DAY 1 LUNCH

Time: 12:00 pm

Food: Turkey and cheese sandwich, carrot sticks, yogurt, grapes, iced tea

DAY 2 LUNCH

Time: 12:20 pm

Food: Spaghetti, sauce, and meatballs, salad, milk

Getting Started

For now, eating consistently is the most important aspect of your food plan. But you'll also want to keep these other tips in mind:

- Eat three moderate-size meals each day. Do not skip meals.

- Eat small between-meal snacks if desired. See page 114 for snack suggestions.

- Eat fewer foods with added sugar, such as regular soft drinks, sugar, syrup, honey, candy, and pie.

- Limit alcohol until you discuss it with your provider. It can affect blood glucose levels.

Of course good nutrition and healthy eating are always important. Eat a variety of healthy foods every day. Include breads and grains, fruits, vegetables, lean meats, and low-fat dairy products. For a healthy heart and weight maintenance, use less fat. Fats include margarine, butter, oil, salad dressing, mayonnaise, nuts, and fried foods.

A NOTE ABOUT WEIGHT

You may notice a small weight gain when you start insulin. This is normal. Your cells are getting back the fluids they need. If you have any questions about this, be sure to ask your provider.

Carbohydrate Foods

The food you eat contains carbohydrate, protein, and fat. Your food plan is focused on carbohydrate foods. Carbohydrate foods include starchy foods like bread and potatoes, fruit, milk, some milk products, and sweets.

Carbohydrate foods are digested and converted into glucose. They make blood glucose levels go up.

But carbohydrate foods are good for you, too. They contain many other important nutrients, vitamins, and minerals. Carbohydrate gives your body energy and supports proper body function.

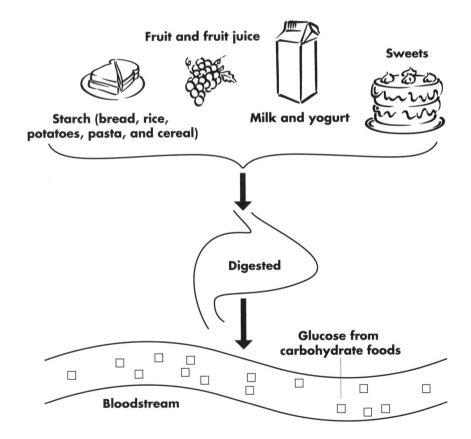

Fruit and fruit juice

Sweets

Starch (bread, rice, potatoes, pasta, and cereal)

Milk and yogurt

Digested

Glucose from carbohydrate foods

Bloodstream

Keeping a Food Record

Before the next session, you need to keep a record of the food you eat for at least three days. This record is a blueprint that will help your dietitian build your personal diabetes food plan.

Write down everything that you eat and drink, even if you don't think it's important. Include how much you eat, too. You might want to measure out your portions, so you can be sure to record the correct amounts.

Your personal eating habits and food choices are worked into your food plan. It's the first step toward better blood glucose control.

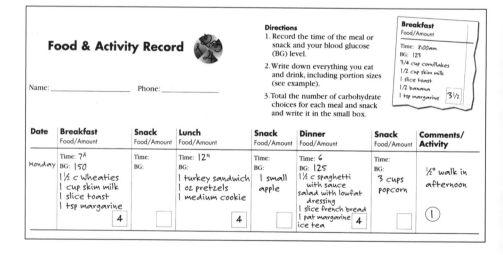

Sample Meals

These meals are examples that show a variety of foods and different portion sizes. Snack examples are listed on page 114.

BREAKFAST

1 cup skim or 1% milk

¾ cup unsweetened cereal

1 slice toast

½ cup orange juice

1 teaspoon soft margarine

LUNCH

2 slices bread

2 ounces turkey

1 cup skim milk

1 apple

1 teaspoon mayonnaise

Lettuce

DINNER

1 medium potato

1 small dinner roll

1 cup skim milk

3-ounce baked chicken breast

½ cup broccoli

1 tablespoon low-fat dressing

1 teaspoon soft margarine

BREAKFAST

1 cup skim or 1% milk

½ cup grits

½ English muffin

½ banana

1 poached egg

LUNCH

2 cups soup (chicken, vegetable, rice)

1 small breadstick

1 slice honeydew melon

Carrot sticks

Iced tea, unsweetened

DINNER

1 cup pasta

½ cup pasta sauce

1 cup skim milk

3 small meatballs, 1 ounce each

1 green salad

1 tablespoon low-fat dressing

Blood Glucose Lows

It is normal for your blood glucose level to go up and down throughout the day. It goes up when you eat. It goes down as your body uses glucose for energy.

Sometimes your blood glucose level can get too low. This is called hypoglycemia. Your heart may beat faster when your blood glucose is low. Other symptoms include:

feeling weak, shaky,
or light-headed

sweaty or clammy skin

irritability

confusion

Whenever you feel symptoms, test your blood glucose level right away. If it is below 80 mg/dL, you need to eat or drink a carbohydrate food (see examples below) to bring it back up. If your number is different from this, your provider will tell you. If you can't test and you feel that your blood glucose is low, go ahead and eat something.

LOW BLOOD GLUCOSE ALERT

If your blood glucose level is _____
(your provider will fill this in)
mg/dL or less, it is too low.
Good choices to eat or drink include one of the following:

- ½ cup orange juice

- 1 cup milk

- ½ cup regular soft drink (not diet)

- 3 or 4 glucose tablets

- 6 Lifesaver® candies

After about 15 minutes, your blood glucose level should go up. Test it again. If it is still too low, eat another carbohydrate food.

Left untreated, hypoglycemia can be dangerous. Always carry some type of carbohydrate with you. This is especially important when you are driving.

Until We Meet Again

- Test your blood glucose and take your insulin every day at the recommended times.

- Test whenever you feel the symptoms of a low blood glucose level.

- Record your test results and insulin doses in your Diabetes Record Book.

- Complete your Food & Activity Record for at least three days before the next session.

- Buy the supplies on the Insulin BASICS Supply List (see page 104).

- Other: _____

YOUR APPOINTMENT FOR SESSION 2 IS:

Day: _____

Date: _____

Time: _____

Place: _____

BRING THE FOLLOWING:

- this book

- your completed Food & Activity Record

- your Diabetes Record Book with recorded test results

- your blood glucose meter, meter instruction manual (if needed), and test strips

- your spouse or significant other

- questions

- other: _____

Welcome

In this session you will:

- learn about the relationship between your food plan and your insulin plan

- learn or review carbohydrate counting

- discover how alcohol affects diabetes control

- learn the effects of physical activity on blood glucose

- evaluate your blood glucose self-test results and learn how to take care of your meter

- learn or review the causes, symptoms, and treatment for hyperglycemia and hypoglycemia

- feel more comfortable with taking insulin

INSULIN BASICS CHECKLIST

Since your last visit, do you have any questions about:

☐ blood glucose testing and targets

☐ measuring and injecting insulin

☐ insulin action times

☐ insulin storage

☐ eating consistently

☐ low blood glucose symptoms and treatment

☐ obtaining diabetes supplies

Your Personal Diabetes Food Plan

Your job for the last several days has been to eat consistently and keep a food record. How did you do? Did you eat at about the same times each day? Did you eat similar kinds and amounts of food at meals? If so, keep up the good work!

Your food record contains a lot of useful information. Your dietitian will use it to develop or refine your personal food plan. It's important to have a food plan that will help you reach your blood glucose targets. It also needs to include nutritious foods that you enjoy.

Your personal food plan usually includes three meals. It may include snacks. It is based on:

- what and when you like to eat

- your lifestyle

- your health needs

Follow your food plan and test your blood glucose levels regularly. Keep accurate food and blood glucose records. This information helps you learn how to keep your blood glucose levels in target.

More About Carbohydrate Foods

You learned that carbohydrate foods are digested and changed into glucose. You also learned that these foods make your blood glucose level go up. But they are not "bad" foods. Remember, our bodies need glucose for energy. And glucose comes from carbohydrate foods.

When you take insulin, you need to match it to the carbohydrate foods you eat. If you don't, your blood glucose level may go too high or too low.

That's why a food plan is so important when designing an insulin plan. The two go together.

Non-carbohydrate foods—such as meats, non-starchy vegetables, and fats—are an important part of your diet. But they have little effect on your blood glucose levels.

✔ QUICK CHECK

Check off the foods that are carbohydrate foods.

☐ Apple   ☐ Mashed potatoes

☐ Steak   ☐ Diet soft drink

☐ Ice cream   ☐ Margarine

☐ Bagel   ☐ Chicken breast

☐ Sour cream   ☐ Pasta

☐ Broccoli   ☐ Peanut butter

☐ Rice   ☐ Orange juice

☐ Skim milk   ☐ Kidney beans

Carbohydrate Counting

Your insulin doses work with the carbohydrate foods you eat to keep your blood glucose levels in target. When the two are matched, your blood glucose level will not go too high or too low. You need to balance your carbohydrate intake with your insulin.

Carbohydrate counting is a way to understand how much carbohydrate you eat. You and your provider then know how much insulin you need to take.

Your food plan includes the amount of carbohydrate you usually eat.

- If you eat more carbohydrate than usual and don't take enough insulin, your blood glucose level will go too high.

- If you don't eat enough carbohydrate to match your insulin dose, or take too much insulin, your blood glucose level will go too low.

What Is a Carbohydrate Choice?

One carbohydrate choice is a serving of food that contains about 15 grams of carbohydrate. Your food plan tells you how many carbohydrate choices you have for each meal and snack. You decide which carbohydrate foods you want to eat.

You need to pay attention to serving sizes in order to count carbohydrates. Your provider or dietitian will give you a list of carbohydrate foods. It will include serving sizes and the number of carbohydrate choices in one serving. If you eat double the serving size listed for a food, you need to count double the carbohydrate choices.

HOW CARBOHYDRATE COUNTING WORKS

Carbohydrate counting allows you to choose what you want to eat. Both of the meals below contain about the same amount of carbohydrate. The foods are different. But each meal counts as four carbohydrate choices.

LUNCH 1	CARBOHYDRATE CHOICES	CARBOHYDRATE GRAMS
1 sandwich (2 slices of bread)	2	30
1 small apple	1	15
1 cup of milk	1	15
TOTAL CARBOHYDRATE	**4 CHOICES**	**60 GRAMS**

LUNCH 2	CARBOHYDRATE CHOICES	CARBOHYDRATE GRAMS
1 cup chili	2	30
6 soda crackers	1	15
½ cup low-fat ice cream	1	15
Green salad with dressing	0	0
TOTAL CARBOHYDRATE	**4 CHOICES**	**60 GRAMS**

Carbohydrate Counting Practice

Figure out how many carbohydrate choices are in each sample meal. You can write in a meal of your own on the next page, if you prefer. Refer to My Food Plan or another list of carbohydrate foods to help you count. Can you figure out the carbohydrate choices for the fast food meal, based on the information you have?

BREAKFAST	AMOUNT	CARBOHYDRATE CHOICES
Orange juice	½ cup	
Cereal, dry	¾ cup	
Milk	½ cup	
Eggs	2	
Toast	1 slice	
Banana	1 medium	
Margarine	1 tsp	
TOTAL CARBOHYDRATE	=	

LUNCH OR DINNER	AMOUNT	CARBOHYDRATE CHOICES
Roast beef	3 oz	
Baked potato	1 medium	
Green beans	½ cup	
Bread roll	1 small	
Butter	1 tsp	
Ice cream	½ cup	
Coffee	1 cup	
TOTAL CARBOHYDRATE	=	

SNACK	AMOUNT	CARBOHYDRATE CHOICES
Popcorn	3 cups	
TOTAL CARBOHYDRATE	**=**	

FAST FOOD MEAL		CARBOHYDRATE CHOICES
Big Mac®		
French fries, large		
16 oz diet soft drink		
Frozen yogurt cone		
TOTAL CARBOHYDRATE	**=**	

MY TYPICAL MEAL	AMOUNT	CARBOHYDRATE CHOICES
TOTAL CARBOHYDRATE	**=**	

Understanding Food Labels

The nutrition labels on food packages are valuable tools. They give all the information you need for carbohydrate counting.

Three pieces of information are especially important:

- Serving size

- Servings per container

- Total carbohydrate (listed in grams for one serving)

Look at the label on the next page, and then take the food label quiz. Use the chart below as a guide for converting carbohydrate grams to carbohydrate choices. Some people prefer to count carbohydrate grams. Use the method that is most comfortable for you. The important thing is that you count.

CARBOHYDRATE GRAMS		CARBOHYDRATE CHOICES
6-10 grams	=	½ choice
15 grams	=	1 choice
30 grams	=	2 choices
45 grams	=	3 choices
60 grams	=	4 choices
75 grams	=	5 choices
90 grams	=	6 choices

FOOD LABEL QUIZ

What is the serving size? _____

How many servings are in this package? _____

How many grams of carbohydrate does one serving contain? ___

One serving counts as _____ carbohydrate choices.

Answers: 1 cup; 2; 31; 2

All the information on the label is based on this portion. If you eat double the serving size, you will eat double the carbohydrate, other nutrients, and calories.

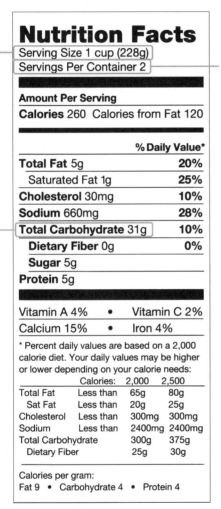

Nutrition Facts

Serving Size 1 cup (228g)
Servings Per Container 2

Amount Per Serving

Calories 260 Calories from Fat 120

	% Daily Value*
Total Fat 5g	**20%**
Saturated Fat 1g	**25%**
Cholesterol 30mg	**10%**
Sodium 660mg	**28%**
Total Carbohydrate 31g	**10%**
Dietary Fiber 0g	**0%**
Sugar 5g	
Protein 5g	

Vitamin A 4%	•	Vitamin C 2%
Calcium 15%	•	Iron 4%

* Percent daily values are based on a 2,000 calorie diet. Your daily values may be higher or lower depending on your calorie needs:

	Calories:	2,000	2,500
Total Fat	Less than	65g	80g
Sat Fat	Less than	20g	25g
Cholesterol	Less than	300mg	300mg
Sodium	Less than	2400mg	2400mg
Total Carbohydrate		300g	375g
Dietary Fiber		25g	30g

Calories per gram:
Fat 9 • Carbohydrate 4 • Protein 4

SERVINGS PER CONTAINER

The number of servings contained in the package.

TOTAL CARBOHYDRATE

The total grams of carbohydrate in one serving. The carbohydrate from dietary fibers and sugar is included in this total, so don't count it twice.

Diabetes and Alcohol

You may have alcohol when you take insulin. But you need to be aware of how it can affect you, and you need to take a few precautions.

Alcohol is not converted into glucose. It is a source of calories that the body must use as energy or store as fat. It can cause weight gain.

Alcohol often lowers blood glucose levels. It then prevents the body from making glucose to bring blood glucose levels up. The result can be hypoglycemia. This is especially true when you take insulin.

The symptoms of hypoglycemia can cause you to appear drunk. It's important for you to wear or carry medical identification at all times. That way, people will know you have diabetes and can get help if you need it.

If you choose to include alcohol in your food plan, follow these simple guidelines:

- Use alcohol only when your diabetes is under control.

- Have it with a meal or snack and not on an empty stomach.

- Limit yourself to one or two drinks per day.

- Wear a diabetes medical identification.

Avoid alcohol if:

- You are pregnant or planning a pregnancy.

- You're trying to lose weight.

- You have high triglycerides (blood fat).

- You have a history of alcohol or other drug abuse.

- You are taking any other medications. Talk to your provider first.

SERVING SIZES OF ALCOHOLIC DRINKS

- 12 ounces regular beer*

- 12 ounces light beer

- 4 ounces dry wine

- 12 ounces wine cooler*

- 1½ ounces scotch, whiskey, gin, etc.

- 2 ounces dry sherry

- ½ ounce liqueur*

- 1 frozen margarita*

Contains significant carbohydrate. Fruit juice, tonic water, and regular soda pop in a mixed drink contains carbohydrate. Non-sweetened mixes are a better choice.

Physical Activity

It's hard to imagine anything better for you than physical activity. This doesn't change when you are taking insulin.

But caution is needed. The most immediate effect of physical activity is to lower blood glucose levels. Active muscles draw glucose out of your bloodstream to use for energy. Your blood glucose level can go too low.

SAFETY TIPS FOR ACTIVITY

- Always carry some form of carbohydrate with you, in case your blood glucose goes too low.

- Test before you begin, if possible. Add more carbohydrate food if you need to. See page 105 for guidelines.

- With type 2, if your blood glucose level is more than 300, monitor your level to see the effects of activity. If your level goes higher, you may need an insulin adjustment.

- With type 1, avoid activity if your blood glucose level is more than 250 mg/dL *and* you have ketones.

- Avoid exercise when you are ill.

While you need to be careful, you can still enjoy all the great benefits of physical activity. These include:

- a feeling of health and well-being, and more energy

- lower blood pressure and improved heart health

- improved strength, endurance, and flexibility

- weight loss or help with weight maintenance

Activity doesn't have to be hard to be good. Everyday things like walking, mowing the lawn, and housework help keep you in good health. They can also lower your blood glucose level.

Use the activity pyramid to decide on ways to include activity in your life. The goal is to work up to thirty minutes of activity, three times per week.

The best activity is one you will do. Choose activities you enjoy. You can do it! Check with your doctor before you begin.

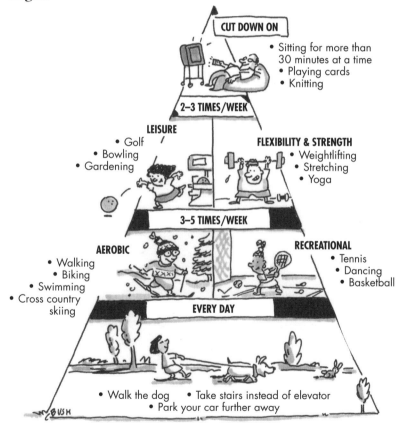

CUT DOWN ON
- Sitting for more than 30 minutes at a time
- Playing cards
- Knitting

2–3 TIMES/WEEK

LEISURE
- Golf
- Bowling
- Gardening

FLEXIBILITY & STRENGTH
- Weightlifting
- Stretching
- Yoga

3–5 TIMES/WEEK

AEROBIC
- Walking
- Biking
- Swimming
- Cross country skiing

RECREATIONAL
- Tennis
- Dancing
- Basketball

EVERY DAY

- Walk the dog
- Take stairs instead of elevator
- Park your car further away

THE ACTIVITY PYRAMID

Adapted from The Activity Pyramid, © *1996 Park Nicollet Institute.*

Insulin and Weight Gain

Many people notice some weight gain when they start taking insulin. Some of this is the result of the body replacing water.

Body cells lose water when blood glucose levels are high. That's why people may lose weight just before being diagnosed with diabetes. People with type 1 diabetes may also lose muscle and fat before diagnosis.

Most people will gain back any recent weight loss once they start taking insulin. If you continue to gain beyond your usual body weight, you may be eating more calories than your body needs.

Continue to take your insulin, even if you gain weight. Maintaining good blood glucose control is the most important thing you can do for your health.

If you wish, you can help limit weight gain by:

- choosing healthy foods

- eating moderate portions

- limiting foods that are high in fat

- exercising regularly

If your weight is an ongoing concern to you, talk to your provider. You can work together to find ways to adjust your food plan or activity level. This will help you lose weight or maintain your current weight.

Getting Comfortable with Insulin

You've had a few days to start getting used to insulin injections. How is it going? Do you feel confident about measuring your insulin? Are you comfortable taking your injections? Is your insulin plan working for you?

It's very important for you to understand the proper way to take insulin. Demonstrate your technique for your provider. Ask questions. Discuss any problems you are having, and be open about your concerns.

It is also important to know how your insulin works. Review the insulin table on page 15. Be sure you understand when each injection you take is working.

Taking insulin as part of your daily routine is a big change in your life. Most people get more comfortable as time goes on. Congratulate yourself for the progress you've made so far!

Complete the following worksheet to find out how well you understand your insulin plan. Ask your provider to help you if you have any questions.

The bolus insulin I take is _____.

It starts to work _____ after I take it.

It works hardest _____ after I take it.

It stops working effectively _____ after I take it.

The background insulin I take is _____.

It starts to work _____ after I take it.

It works hardest _____ after I take it.

It stops working effectively _____ after I take it.

I keep open insulin (check all that apply):

☐ In the refrigerator

☐ In a cupboard or medicine cabinet

☐ In my purse, briefcase, or pocket

☐ In my desk at work

☐ Another place (explain) _____

I keep unopened insulin (check all that apply):

☐ In the refrigerator

☐ In a cupboard or medicine cabinet

☐ In my purse, briefcase, or pocket

☐ In my desk at work

☐ Another place (explain) _____

I carry _____ with me to eat, in case my blood glucose level goes too low.

Making Sure Your Meter Works

Your blood glucose test results help you and your provider make decisions about your treatment. It's important that these results are accurate.

To ensure accurate test results, your blood glucose meter needs a little upkeep. Follow the steps below to make sure it keeps working properly.

1. Be sure the code number on your meter matches the code number on your test strips.

2. Be sure you obtain a drop of blood large enough for your meter to read accurately.

3. Check your meter with control solution when opening a new vial of test strips. Check also if you get a test result that doesn't seem right to you.

4. If your meter has a calibration check strip, use it as directed.

5. Check your meter book for instructions on how to keep it clean.

Call the manufacturer's toll-free number on the back of your meter if you have questions or concerns about it.

Working Toward Control

Look at the test results you wrote in your Diabetes Record Book. If your blood glucose levels are not in the target range, changes in your insulin doses may be needed.

Your goal is to have at least one-half (50%) of your readings in range. Don't be discouraged if you're not there yet. It can take several weeks or more to accomplish this goal.

You and your provider will keep working to bring your blood glucose levels into range. Your job is to continue to test and record your blood glucose level four times a day. You need to test:

- before breakfast
- before lunch
- before dinner
- before going to bed

You may need to test at other times as well. Your provider will tell you if you do.

Blood Glucose Highs

You may be feeling better now that you are taking insulin. This means that your blood glucose levels are moving closer to your target range.

Many people, however, continue to have symptoms. For example, you might still feel tired or have blurry vision. These symptoms should improve as your blood glucose levels continue to come down.

If your blood glucose levels are not coming down, your insulin doses may need to be changed. They may also need to be changed if you have altered your eating habits or activity level.

A blood glucose level of 250 mg/dL or higher can signal a problem. You may need to check your urine for ketones. Ketones are a sign that your body is burning fat for energy. This can be dangerous, particularly in type 1 diabetes.

As long as your blood glucose level is high, you need to check for ketones about every four hours. Call your provider if you have a moderate to large amount of ketones two tests in a row.

CAUSES OF HIGH BLOOD GLUCOSE

- Eating more food or being less active than usual
- Being under physical or emotional stress
- Not taking enough diabetes medication (insulin/pills)
- Taking insulin that is expired or hasn't been stored properly
- Being ill

Blood Glucose Lows

When you take insulin, your blood glucose level may go too low at times. Can you name the main symptoms of low blood glucose, or hypoglycemia? Review the symptoms and causes of hypoglycemia and how to treat it on pages 32–33.

You can prevent low blood glucose levels, once you know what causes them. Remember that insulin brings blood glucose levels down. Carbohydrate brings them up.

When you have too much insulin compared to carbohydrate, your blood glucose can go too low. You need to eat enough carbohydrate to match the insulin doses you take. Don't skip meals or snacks that are part of your food plan.

Physical activity also lowers blood glucose levels. If you are going to be very active, you may need to eat extra carbohydrate to counter the effect. Talk to your provider if you have questions.

A dangerously low blood glucose level can cause seizures or unconsciousness. If that happens, it's very important for people to know that you have diabetes. Wear or carry a diabetes medical identification at all times. That way people will know what to do to help you.

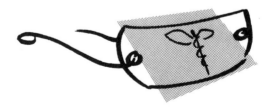

LOWS THAT AREN'T REALLY LOWS

Sometimes you may have symptoms even though your blood glucose is not low. This can happen if your level drops a lot (more than 100 mg/dL) in a short period of time. Your body may respond to the rapid change just as if you were having a true low.

It is best not to treat the symptoms unless your blood glucose level is below 80 mg/dL. If you cannot test and you feel low, treat the symptoms. Eat or drink something containing 15 grams of carbohydrate. See page 33 for a list of convenient foods for treating low blood glucose.

USE CAUTION WHEN DRIVING

It is especially important to have a carbohydrate source with you when you are driving. It is also a good idea to test your blood glucose level before you get behind the wheel. If it's low, eat a carbohydrate food and retest before you go.

If you feel low while you are driving, pull over to the side of the road. Test your blood glucose and eat a carbohydrate food if it is low. Wait for your blood glucose level to go up before you get back on the road.

CAUSES OF LOW BLOOD GLUCOSE

- Eating less food than usual, particularly carbohydrate food

- Skipping or delaying a meal or snack

- Getting more exercise than usual

- Taking too much insulin or diabetes medication

Severe Blood Glucose Lows

A low blood glucose level needs to be treated with some form of glucose. If it's not treated, severe hypoglycemia may develop.

Anytime you need someone else's help to treat a low blood glucose level, it is considered severe. Sometimes this is called an insulin reaction.

Severe blood glucose lows can cause you to become confused, act strangely, have convulsions, or even lose consciousness. You may refuse the food that people offer you. Or you may be unable to eat or drink.

To treat a severe low, someone else needs to inject you with a substance called glucagon. You need to keep glucagon handy at home and anywhere you spend a lot of time. Your family and people close to you need to know how to use it properly. It is a safe medication that your provider will prescribe for you.

HOW TO GIVE GLUCAGON

1. Mix the glucagon and draw it into the syringe as instructed in the glucagon kit.

2. Inject the glucagon into fatty tissue (the same places insulin is injected).

3. Wait fifteen minutes for the glucagon to work.

4. If there is no improvement, call 911.

After receiving glucagon, you need to eat or drink small amounts of a carbohydrate food. Regular soft drinks, soda crackers, and dry toast are good choices. Start as soon as you are alert enough to swallow. Continue to eat or drink slowly until your blood glucose level is above 70 mg/dL.

Contact your provider after any treatment with glucagon. You can work together to determine what caused the severe low. You may need to make changes in your insulin doses to prevent it from happening again.

Test your blood glucose level at least four times a day for two days after a severe low. Call your provider if you continue to have low readings.

TIPS FOR USING GLUCAGON

- Make sure the people close to you know how to inject glucagon. Periodically review the instructions in the glucagon kit with them.

- If glucagon is mixed but not used, throw it away. It cannot be saved to use at another time.

- Check the expiration date on your glucagon box regularly. Replace it before it expires. Expired glucagon won't help you in an emergency.

Until We Meet Again

- Test your blood glucose and take your insulin every day at the recommended times.

- Test whenever you feel the symptoms of a low blood glucose level.

- Record your test results and insulin doses in your Diabetes Record Book.

- Complete your Food & Activity Record for at least three days before the next session.

- Other: _____

YOUR APPOINTMENT FOR SESSION 3 IS:

Day: _____

Date: _____

Time: _____

Place: _____

BRING THE FOLLOWING:

- this book

- your completed Food & Activity Record

- your Diabetes Record Book with recorded test results

- your blood glucose meter and test strips

- your spouse or significant other

- questions

- other: _____

Welcome

In this session you will:

- evaluate your blood glucose test results

- learn to recognize blood glucose patterns

- learn when and how to adjust insulin to correct patterns

- learn to adjust carbohydrate intake for physical activity

- learn how illness affects blood glucose control and what to do when you are ill

- develop personal action goals

- feel affirmed in your efforts to manage your diabetes

INSULIN BASICS CHECKLIST

Since your last visit, do you have any questions about:

☐ blood glucose testing times and targets

☐ measuring and injecting insulin

☐ carbohydrate counting or label reading

☐ the effects of alcohol on blood glucose

☐ the effects of physical activity on blood glucose

☐ blood glucose highs or lows

☐ using glucagon for severe hypoglycemia

Record Book Review

Your goal is to have at least one-half (50%) of your blood glucose test results within the target range. When you reach this goal, your HbA$_{1c}$ should be in target, too. Look back to page 13 to see your HbA$_{1c}$ target.

Look at the test results you recorded in your Diabetes Record Book for the last two weeks. Highlight the numbers in your target range. Fill in the blanks below.

TESTS IN TARGET RANGE	TOTAL NUMBER OF TESTS	% TESTS WITHIN TARGET
_____ ÷	_____ =	_____

Divide the number of tests within target by the total number of tests. Are at least 50% (0.5 or higher) of your blood glucose tests within target?

When you first start taking insulin, reaching your goal may take awhile. You and your provider will keep working to bring your blood glucose levels into range. Several adjustments may be needed to find the right insulin doses for you. Stick with it!

Continue to test and record your blood glucose level four times a day. You need to test:

- before breakfast

- before lunch

- before dinner

- before going to bed

You may need to test at other times as well. Your provider will tell you if you do.

Insulin Plan Review

You and your provider have probably made some adjustments to your insulin doses. You may have added an injection or changed the time of an injection. In the process, you've learned some things about how insulin works. You know that:

- Insulin works with carbohydrates to give you energy.

- Different kinds of insulin work differently in the body.

- You need to match your insulin doses to the carbohydrate you eat.

The next step is to learn how and why insulin dose adjustments are made. To learn this, you need to understand how your insulin and food plans work together.

Look at the information you've written in your record book. When is your insulin working hardest? Which meals or snacks does each injection cover? Which insulin doses affect each of your blood glucose readings? If you need a reminder, review the insulin action times on page 15.

✔ QUICK CHECK

Sometimes you need to test your blood glucose beyond your usual testing schedule. Check off other times you may need to test:

☐ Before you drive

☐ After eating a salad

☐ Before physical activity

☐ After physical activity

☐ After treating a low

☐ After you eat at a new restaurant

☐ When you are bored

☐ When you feel symptoms of a low blood glucose level

Blood Glucose Patterns

One approach to insulin dose adjustments is called pattern control. A pattern is a series of blood glucose readings taken at the same time each day that are outside your target range. For example, the record book below shows a pattern of highs before dinner. A true pattern occurs every day for three or more days in a row.

TARGET: 80–140 mg/dL

Date	3 AM BG	BREAKFAST BG	Med	BG	LUNCH BG	Med	BG	DINNER BG	Med	BG	BEDTIME BG	Med
10-6		128	12 LIS/ 10 ULT		140	8 LIS	157	(234)	14 LIS		147	22 NPH
10-7		117	"		135	"	141	(146)	"		123	"
10-8		136	"		156	"	171	(239)	"		138	"

LIS = Lispro   ULT = Ultralente

When you see a pattern in your record book, it means that a change is needed. It might be a change in your carbohydrate intake, your insulin dose, or your activity level. Changing any one of these will affect your blood glucose.

Remember that carbohydrate makes blood glucose levels go up. So reducing the amount of carbohydrate in your food plan may help correct a pattern of high blood glucose levels. Insulin and activity both bring blood glucose levels down. So you would need *more* insulin or activity to help correct a pattern of highs.

✔ QUICK CHECK

How do changes in your carbohydrate intake, insulin doses, and activity affect your blood glucose levels? Check one box for each change.

Change	Blood Glucose Goes Up	Blood Glucose Goes Down
Eat more carbohydrate food	☐	☐
Eat less carbohydrate food	☐	☐
Be more active	☐	☐
Be less active	☐	☐
Take more insulin	☐	☐
Take less insulin	☐	☐

Making Insulin Dose Adjustments

Insulin dose adjustments are a very effective method for correcting blood glucose patterns. Many people prefer it to changing their carbohydrate intake or activity level.

It may seem a little scary to change your insulin dose yourself. But you can learn to do it safely. You just need to have a few things in place first.

Do you:

- know your blood glucose target range?   ☐ Yes ☐ No

- count carbohydrates and eat consistently?   ☐ Yes ☐ No

- test and record your blood glucose levels regularly?   ☐ Yes ☐ No

- know which insulin dose affects each of your blood glucose readings?   ☐ Yes ☐ No

- understand how physical activity affects your blood glucose levels?   ☐ Yes ☐ No

If you answered "yes" to all of these questions, you are probably ready to try adjusting insulin. If you are unsure, talk it over with your provider.

Determining Which Dose to Adjust

There are two parts to determining which dose to adjust to correct a blood glucose pattern. You need to know:

- which injection is causing the pattern

- which insulin in that injection is causing the pattern

The first part is easy. What is the last injection you took prior to the pattern? This is the injection that is the most likely cause of the pattern. For example, the injection you take at dinner could cause a pattern before bedtime.

The second part—which insulin is causing the pattern—depends on your insulin plan. You need to adjust the insulin that is working at the time of the pattern.

Use the table to help determine which insulin to adjust.

FOR A BLOOD GLUCOSE PATTERN AT THIS TIME...	YOU MAY NEED TO ADJUST THIS INSULIN DOSE...
Before breakfast	Dinner or bedtime background insulin
Before lunch	Breakfast short-acting insulin or Breakfast background insulin or Bedtime long-acting insulin
Before dinner	Lunch short-acting insulin or Breakfast background insulin or Bedtime long-acting insulin
Before bedtime snack	Dinner short-acting insulin or Bedtime long-acting insulin
3 a.m.	Dinner or bedtime background insulin or Bedtime long-acting insulin
2 hours after the start of a meal	Rapid-acting insulin from the previous meal

Deciding How to Adjust

Once you've determined which insulin you need to adjust, you can take action to correct the pattern. Change only one kind of insulin and one dose at a time. If there are patterns of both highs and lows, correct the lows first. This will help prevent hypoglycemia. After the lows are corrected, adjust for highs if necessary.

- If you are correcting a pattern of readings that are too low, *decrease* the appropriate insulin dose.

- If you are correcting a pattern of readings that are too high, *increase* the appropriate insulin dose.

The amount of the adjustment is based on the amount of your current dose. Generally, if you take higher doses you can adjust in greater increments.

To start out, it's best to adjust by only one or two units of insulin at a time. Never adjust by more than two units at a time. Talk to your provider about how much to adjust.

CURRENT DOSE	PATTERN OF LOWS	PATTERN OF HIGHS
10 units or less	Decrease by 1 unit	Increase by 1 unit
More than 10 units	Decrease by 2 units	Increase by 2 units

Look at the record book example and answer the questions.

TARGET RANGE: 80–140 MG/DL
REGIMEN: 12 LIS/24 NPH — 0 — 10 LIS — 14 NPH

Date	3 AM BG	BREAKFAST			LUNCH			DINNER			BEDTIME	
		BG	Med	BG	BG	Med	BG	BG	Med	BG	BG	Med
Mon		120	12 LIS/ 24 NPH		92			66	10 LIS		104	14 NPH
Tues		96	"		73			64	"		102	"
Wed		85	"		89			58	"		113	"

LIS = Lispro

1. Do you see a pattern? If so, what is it?

   _____

2. Which insulin dose would you adjust to correct the
   pattern? _____

3. Would you increase or decrease the dose?

   _____

4. By how much?

   _____

67

Using Other Medications

Certain non-diabetes medications can affect your blood glucose. For example, steroids (such as prednisone or cortisone), diuretics, and estrogen may cause your blood glucose level to go up.

Some over-the-counter medications, such as cough syrup, contain sugar. These can also cause blood glucose highs.

Always read the labels of non-prescription medications. Check for warnings for people with diabetes. Ask your provider or pharmacist if you have any questions.

When you start a new medication for another health problem:

- ask your provider how it might affect your blood glucose

- write the date you start it in your Diabetes Record Book. This will help you track any changes in your blood glucose levels.

- you may need an insulin adjustment if your blood glucose levels change. Check with your provider.

Food Plan Review

It's a good idea to check in with yourself regularly about your eating habits. Most people have a mixture of successes and challenges with following a food plan. How is it going for you? Are you counting carbohydrates?

Take time to feel good about the things that are going well. You're doing a great job!

If you find that you are having difficulties, try to pinpoint problem areas. Think of ways to improve in these areas.

Be kind to yourself as you work on changing behaviors. Don't expect to do everything perfectly. But keep trying!

More on Physical Activity

In Session 2, you learned about the importance and benefits of physical activity. It improves your overall health. It can help you lose or maintain weight.

When you take insulin, physical activity can also cause low blood glucose levels. But that's no reason not to be active! You just need to plan ahead to prevent any problems.

There are two things you can do to keep your blood glucose level from getting too low:

- You can eat more carbohydrate.

- You can lower your insulin dose.

To start out, it's better to eat more carbohydrate when you are going to be more active than usual. (See page 105 of the Appendix for guidelines on adding carbohydrate for physical activity.) Later on, when you are comfortable taking insulin, you can learn to adjust your doses.

SAFETY TIPS FOR PHYSICAL ACTIVITY

- Test your blood glucose before and one hour after a new activity. This will help you learn what effect it has on your blood glucose levels.

- If your blood glucose level is below your target range after activity, eat or drink more carbohydrate the next time. (See page 105.)

- Begin your activity after your insulin dose is past its peak action time. See page 15 to review insulin action times.

You can usually add one carbohydrate choice for each hour of moderate activity. For example, for an hour of walking, drink a small glass (½ cup) of orange juice. It contains about 15 grams of carbohydrate. Also, be sure to carry a carbohydrate choice with you, such as glucose tablets.

The food you eat to prevent low blood glucose levels is added to your usual food plan. It does not replace the carbohydrate choices you usually have for meals and snacks.

Remember to always carry a carbohydrate source with you during any physical activity in case you feel low.

✔ QUICK CHECK

Which of the following foods are good choices to carry with you in case your blood glucose gets too low?

☐ 12 carrot sticks   ☐ 3 glucose tabs

☐ 1 granola bar   ☐ Small bag of peanuts

☐ Protein drink, 8 ounces   ☐ 1 juice box, 4 ounces

☐ Bottled water, 8 ounces   ☐ 1 beef jerky stick

☐ Small bag of pretzels

When You Are Sick

You need to pay special attention to your diabetes during an illness like a cold or the flu. Illness puts stress on your body and can cause high blood glucose levels. In fact, high levels can be the first sign that you might be coming down with something.

Blood glucose can get high very fast when you're sick. Be sure to take your normal doses of insulin, even if you are eating very little.

Test and record your blood glucose level every two to four hours. If you have type 1 diabetes, check for ketones at least every four hours.

Call your provider if:

- Most of your blood glucose test results are over 250 mg/dL for three days in a row.

- Your blood glucose level falls below 70 mg/dL more than once during your illness.

- You are vomiting.

- You have persistent diarrhea.

- You have moderate to large ketones in your urine.

- You have acute abdominal pain.

- You are having difficulty breathing (a symptom of too many ketones in the blood).

- You feel you want to change your insulin doses during an illness.

Your body needs fuel to help with healing. Even though blood glucose levels can go up during illness, you still need to eat and drink.

Be sure to eat foods or drink liquids that contain carbohydrate. If you feel sick to your stomach, choose foods that you think will stay down. It's okay to have regular soft drinks, ice cream, or other sweets at these times.

Try to have one carbohydrate choice (15 grams of carbohydrate) for each hour that you are awake. If you can eat more, follow your usual food plan.

CARBOHYDRATE CHOICES FOR SICK DAYS

- ½ cup regular soft drink
- 6 saltine crackers
- 1 slice toast
- 1 cup soup (not broth)
- ½ cup sweetened gelatin
- 1 Popsicle (60 to 80 calories)
- ½ cup ice cream or frozen yogurt
- 1 tablespoon honey or sugar in tea
- ¼ cup sherbet or fruit ice

Drink plenty of sugar-free liquids to help replace the body fluids you lose during an illness. Examples include water, broth, and tea. Sipping liquids slowly will help them stay down if you are feeling sick to your stomach.

Setting Personal Goals

By now you know that staying healthy with diabetes means making some changes in your lifestyle. For example, you may need to:

- test your blood glucose level more often

- record your test results regularly

- eat carbohydrate foods in a more consistent manner

- become more physically active

Setting a goal for yourself can help you make the changes you need to make. You know best what those changes are.

SAMPLE GOALS

- I will take my insulin at the scheduled times every day.

- I will eat a consistent amount of carbohydrate at dinner every day.

- I will carry glucose tablets with me when I go for my walk.

An effective goal needs to be both reasonable and measurable. A reasonable goal reflects your current health and abilities. It is something within your reach. A measurable goal is specific, not open-ended. It states what you will do and when you will do it.

A goal needs checkpoints for evaluating progress. A goal also deserves your commitment. Commitment turns something you feel you should do into something you believe you will do.

Think about what changes you want to make. Try to write at least one reasonable and measurable goal that you would like to work on.

REASONABLE	UNREASONABLE
An inactive person writes, "I will walk for twenty minutes, three days a week, for the next two months."	An inactive person writes, "I will jog three miles five days a week."

MEASURABLE	NOT MEASURABLE
"I will drink 1% milk instead of whole milk for the next three months."	"I will eat better from now on."

Until We Meet Again

- Test your blood glucose and take your insulin every day at the recommended times.

- Test whenever you feel the symptoms of a low blood glucose level.

- Record your test results and insulin doses in your Diabetes Record Book.

- Complete your Food & Activity Record for at least three days before the next session.

- Work on the goal you set for yourself.

- Other: _____

YOUR APPOINTMENT FOR SESSION 4 IS:

Day: _____

Date: _____

Time: _____

Place: _____

BRING THE FOLLOWING:

- this book

- your completed Food & Activity Record

- your Diabetes Record Book with recorded test results

- your copy of My Personal Goals Action Plan

- your blood glucose meter and test strips

- your spouse or significant other

- questions

- other: _____

Welcome

In this session you will:

- understand HbA_{1c} as a measure of blood glucose control

- recognize the importance of caring for your feet

- learn what to expect from your healthcare provider

- learn strategies for dining out and meal time changes

- discover strategies for healthy eating and lowering heart disease risk

- learn how stress affects blood glucose

- understand the need for continuing diabetes education

- better appreciate your ability to self-manage your diabetes

INSULIN BASICS CHECKLIST:

Since your last visit, do you have any questions about:

☐ your HbA_{1c}

☐ identifying blood glucose patterns

☐ making insulin adjustments

☐ making carbohydrate adjustments for physical activity

☐ using non-diabetes medications

☐ sick-day management

☐ personal action goals

Keeping Blood Glucose Levels in Target

You've probably made a lot of changes in your life over the past several weeks. You're testing your blood glucose levels and taking your insulin injections. You may be more active than you used to be.

You've been making changes to help keep your blood glucose levels in target. How have you been doing? Are at least one-half of your blood glucose tests within target? If so, good for you! Celebrate your success and keep it up. If they're not, you and your provider will work together to figure out why. Then you can do something about it.

Your HbA_{1c} is another way to track your progress toward blood glucose control. Be sure to have an HbA_{1c} test every three to four months.

You may or may not have reached your HbA_{1c} target yet. But any improvement means that you are on your way to better health. You can check back on page 13 to review your HbA_{1c} target.

Look at the test results you recorded in your Diabetes Record Book for the last two weeks. Highlight the numbers in your target range. Fill in the blanks below.

TESTS IN TARGET RANGE	**TOTAL NUMBER OF TESTS**	**% TESTS WITHIN TARGET**

_____ ÷ _____ = _____

Divide the number of tests within target by the total number of tests. Are at least 50% (0.5 or higher) of your blood glucose tests within target?

Continue to test and record your blood glucose level four times a day. You need to test:

- before breakfast

- before lunch

- before dinner

- before going to bed

You may need to test at other times as well. Your provider will tell you if you do.

Pattern Control Review

In Session 3, you learned how to recognize blood glucose patterns. You also learned how to make insulin adjustments to correct patterns.

You may or may not feel comfortable making insulin adjustments at this time. Remember that you can also correct patterns by changing your food intake or physical activity level. You can eat more carbohydrate to correct a pattern of lows. You can eat less carbohydrate or increase your physical activity to correct a pattern of highs.

Look at the record book example and answer the questions.

TARGET RANGE: 80–140 MG/DL
REGIMEN: 8 LIS — 6 LIS — 10 LIS — 24 GLA

Date	3 AM BG	BREAKFAST			LUNCH			DINNER			BEDTIME	
		BG	Med	BG	BG	Med	BG	BG	Med	BG	BG	Med
Mon		114	8 LIS	188	148	6 LIS		137	10 LIS		126	24 GLA
Tues		98	"	192	152	"		123	"		139	"
Wed		127	"	203	160	"		143	"		152	"

LIS=Lispro; GLA=Glargine

1. What pattern do you see? _____

2. Why were blood glucose tests done two hours after breakfast? _____

3. What do these tests tell you? _____

4. Which insulin dose would you adjust and by how much?

_____

Five Steps to Healthy Feet

One more reason to keep your blood glucose levels in target is your feet. That may sound funny, but think about it. High blood glucose levels affect your heart and circulation. Where's the farthest your blood has to travel in your body? Your feet!

Poor circulation and nerve damage usually affect the feet and lower legs first. You might feel numbness, tingling, or pain. You might have sores that won't heal.

These problems can become very serious. You need to take care of your feet every day to prevent this from happening. Follow the five steps for healthy feet on the next page.

FOOT-CARE GUIDELINES

- Wear shoes at all times.

- Keep your feet dry. (Don't soak them.)

- Avoid using chemical treatments, sharp instruments, sandpaper, or pumice to treat calluses, corns, or other foot problems.

- Keep your feet protected from extreme heat or cold.

- Avoid heating pads or hot water bottles on your feet.

- Cross you legs at the ankle, not your knee.

- Break in a new pair of shoes by wearing them for short periods of time—not all day.

Step 1: Keep your blood glucose levels in target. We've already said a lot about this. The best way to stay healthy and prevent problems is to control blood glucose levels.

Step 2: Practice good foot-care habits. Wash your feet with mild soap and water every day. Dry them completely. Trim toenails straight across. Use lotion if your skin is dry, but don't get lotion between your toes. Wear socks and shoes made from natural materials such as cotton, wool, and leather. Make sure your toes have room to wiggle in your shoes.

Step 3: Check your feet daily. Look them over thoroughly—top, bottom, and between your toes. Use a mirror to check hard-to-see places. Look for corns and calluses, ingrown nails, cuts, blisters, or cracked skin. If you notice any sign of infection, call your provider. Signs of infection include redness, red streaks, swelling, oozing, warm spots, and pain.

Step 4: Treat foot injuries immediately. Minor blisters, cuts, or scrapes can be cleaned and treated with antibiotic cream. Check daily to make sure the area is healing. Stay alert for signs of infection. If you're unsure how to treat a foot injury, call your provider.

Step 5: Visit your provider every three to four months. Remove your shoes and socks to ensure that your feet are examined at every visit. Discuss any problems or questions you have. Ask if you need and qualify for prescription footwear.

Staying Healthy for a Lifetime

You need to care for your diabetes every day. You also need to visit your provider about every three to four months. You and your provider will review your blood glucose records and laboratory test results. You will discuss your treatment plan and any changes that may be needed.

The Physical Tune-up on pages 108–109 is a one-year schedule for keeping track of your diabetes care visits. It shows all the tests and exams you can expect to have and the target for each. If you have questions about your care, be sure to ask your provider.

Regular diabetes care visits help you stay in control of your diabetes and your blood glucose levels. High blood glucose levels over a period of time can lead to serious health complications.

Diabetes complications can affect the eyes, the heart, the kidneys, the feet, and sexual function in men. Research has shown that blood glucose control helps prevent, delay, or slow the progression of diabetes complications.

BLOOD GLUCOSE CONTROL REDUCES THE RISK OF...	BY...
Eye problems	76%
Heart disease	42%
Kidney disease	56%
Nerve damage	60%

Data from the 10-year Diabetes Control and Complications Trial concluded in 1993 and the United Kingdom Prospective Diabetes Study, which ended in 1999.

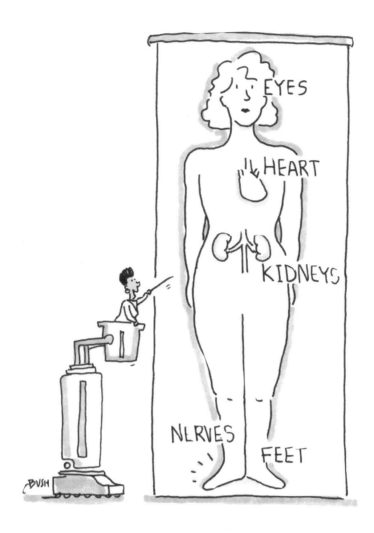

You need to take charge of your diabetes to give yourself the best chance of avoiding complications.

One of the best things you can do for yourself is to stop smoking. The combination of smoking and diabetes is especially deadly.

Nicotine is a highly addictive drug. Quitting can be very hard. But if you are ready to try, your provider can help you find a program or treatment. Your health may depend on it!

The Keys to Food Plan Success

Diabetes truly affects every part of your life. That's why it's so important for you to learn about diabetes and food planning. The more you know, the more successful you'll be at living well with diabetes.

Two important keys to success in food planning are:

- accurately estimating portion sizes

- counting carbohydrates

Once you learn these skills you can eat anywhere with confidence. You will know how to follow your food plan in any situation.

You need to know the portion size of the food you want to eat in order to know how much carbohydrate you are eating. This helps keep your blood glucose levels in target.

You could measure your food servings, but that's not always possible. Instead you need to learn to estimate portions by sight.

FOOD AND AMOUNT	SERVING-SIZE SHORTCUT
½ medium fruit	= tennis ball
1 4-inch pancake	= compact disk (CD)
1 ounce chips or pretzels	= 1 heaping handful
½ cup mashed potatoes	= cupcake wrapper

Estimating portions can be tricky. Try practicing at home. Look at what ½ cup of mashed potatoes looks like on a dinner plate. Put the same amount in a bowl. Now try it with 1 cup of mashed potatoes. Can you see the difference?

Weigh a 3 ounce baked potato. This is one carbohydrate choice. If the potato you plan to eat is bigger, then it counts as more than one choice.

After awhile you'll be able to dish up the serving size you want without measuring. But check yourself once in awhile. When you're estimating portions, they tend to grow over time.

And why are portions so important? Because you need to count the carbohydrate you are eating. Remember, when you eat double the portion size, you need to count the carbohydrate twice.

✔ QUICK CHECK

Using your list of carbohydrate foods, create a meal with four carbohydrate choices.

MENU	AMOUNT	CARBOHYDRATE CHOICES
TOTAL CARBOHYDRATE	**= 4 CHOICES**	

Strategies for Dining Out

Eating at a restaurant used to be a luxury. Today many of us eat at restaurants regularly. This does not have to change just because you are taking insulin.

You can enjoy eating away from home and still maintain good blood glucose control. Select foods and portions that equal the carbohydrate choices in your food plan. Take the time to practice measuring food portions at home. It will help you learn how to "eyeball" them when you're away.

Remember that your insulin doses are designed to match your carbohydrate choices. You can't "save" carbohydrate choices from one meal and have them at another. You need to follow your food plan for the meal you are eating out.

The chart on pages 106–107 shows the carbohydrate choices for some popular restaurant menu items. Smart, lower-fat choices are marked with a ♥. Use the chart and the guidelines below to have a healthy dining experience.

Know your portions. Restaurant portions are usually large. Learn to estimate appropriate serving sizes when dining out. You can also take clues from your Diabetes Record Book. If you see your levels are always high after pasta meals, double-check your portion the next time. Were you counting correctly?

Watch the fat. Restaurant food often has a lot of added fat. Look for broiled, baked, grilled, or steamed menu items. Remove skin from poultry and trim fat from meat. It's okay to save up fat servings to use for a special meal.

Ask for what you want. Request that food be prepared with less fat. Get salad dressing "on the side," and butter your own potato. You'll probably use less if you add it yourself. Try substituting a salad or a baked potato for French fries.

Enjoy yourself! If you overindulge, don't panic. A little exercise can help make up for a carbohydrate splurge. Take a walk or go dancing to balance things out. If you find that you overeat often, try to plan ahead. Develop strategies for avoiding temptation, such as having a salad before a pizza meal.

When You Can't Eat on Time

With busy schedules and family activities, it's not always possible to eat at the same times every day. You may work different shifts, travel often, or have frequent schedule changes. You may need to delay a meal. There are ways to work around this when you are taking insulin.

If you take only bolus insulin before the meal, it's easy. Take your insulin when you're ready to eat. Regular insulin needs to be taken 30 minutes before the meal. Lispro and Aspart insulin need to be taken immediately before you eat.

If you take both bolus and background insulin before the meal, you need to consider how long your meal will be delayed.

FOR DELAYS LESS THAN 1½ HOURS

- Wait and take your usual insulin injection when you are ready to eat.

- If you've already taken your insulin, have one carbohydrate choice to help prevent a low-blood glucose level.

FOR DELAYS LONGER THAN 1½ HOURS

- Take your background insulin at the usual time. Then take your bolus insulin just before the meal.

- Or just take your usual insulin injection when you are ready to eat

Ask your provider which option is the better one for you.

When You Want to Eat More or Less

Occasionally you may want to eat "outside your food plan." You may want to eat more or less carbohydrate than usual.

You can adjust the dose of your bolus insulin (Regular, Lispro, or Aspart) to prevent high or low blood glucose levels. Remember, your insulin dose needs to "match" the carbohydrate foods in your meal.

Before you start adjusting your insulin doses, you need to:

- have at least half of your blood glucose readings in target

- count carbohydrates regularly and accurately

- understand how your insulin works

- understand the causes of blood glucose highs and lows

- know how to look for patterns in your record book

The amount of insulin you adjust depends on your individual plan. You will add or subtract a certain amount of insulin for each carbohydrate choice you add or subtract. That amount is called your insulin-to-carbohydrate ratio.

If you feel ready to start adjusting insulin for food, ask your provider to help you determine your insulin-to-carbohydrate ratio.

If you are trying to lose or maintain weight, use caution. Adding extra food and insulin can lead to weight gain.

••

I need to adjust my bolus insulin by _____ units for each carbohydrate choice I add or subtract.

The Food Pyramid

By now, you're probably an expert at carbohydrate counting. You know that the insulin you take is matched to the carbohydrate foods that you eat. You also know that this leads to healthy blood glucose levels.

It's also important for you to include a variety of foods in your diet. This helps you get all the nutrients you need for good health. It also helps prevent "food boredom," which can lead to unhealthy eating behaviors.

The Food Pyramid is an excellent guide to healthful eating. It divides foods into six main groups. It also tells you the number of servings you need from each group every day for good nutrition.

The carbohydrate food groups are shaded in light gray in the pyramid. Many healthy and delicious foods are carbohydrate foods. Just remember that the insulin doses you take need to match the number of carbohydrate choices you eat. So don't forget to count them!

Fats/Sweets/Alcohol
Use Sparingly

Milk/Yogurt
2–3 servings
each day

Meat/Meat Substitutes
2–3 servings
each day

Vegetables
3–5 servings
each day

Fruits
3–4 servings
each day

Grains/Beans/Starchy Vegetables
6 or more servings each day

Healthy Heart Habits

Heart health is important because diabetes increases your risk for heart disease. It also increases your risk of developing high blood cholesterol, high triglycerides (blood fats), and high blood pressure. All of these contribute to heart disease.

The good news is that everything you do to control your blood glucose levels also helps keep your heart healthy. But you may need to do more.

Healthy heart habits include making wise food choices. Two big enemies of heart health are fast food and junk food. These foods are often very high in fat. Use the lists of healthy snacks and restaurant foods in the Appendix to make good food choices.

Other lifestyle behaviors also help improve your heart health and reduce your risk for heart disease. Follow these guidelines:

- choose low-fat foods and use low-fat cooking methods (bake, broil, boil, or steam)

- eat fewer salty foods and avoid using the salt shaker

- cut down on alcohol

- make physical activity a part of your daily routine

- maintain a healthy weight

- stop smoking

- take a low dose of aspirin daily if recommended by your provider

Balancing Stress

Stress can make blood glucose levels hard to control. Both negative and positive events can cause stress. Illness, moving, marriage, retirement—all are stressful.

Stress can also interfere with your diabetes care schedule. Then it's even harder to keep blood glucose levels in target. And that causes more stress!

The Balancing Stress Pyramid shows ways to keep your life balanced. Decide what works for you. And try to follow your treatment plan, especially during stressful times.

My diabetes
is out of control!

I'm so stressed!

I don't feel like exercising!

BUSH

Balancing Stress Pyramid

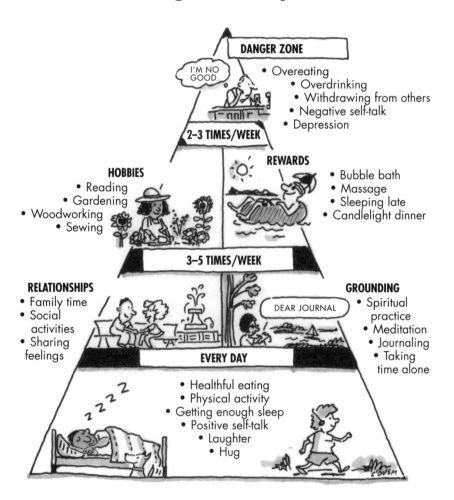

Personal Goals Checkpoint

It's time to check in with your personal goals. How do you think you're doing?

If you're doing well, congratulate yourself! Commit to continuing your healthy behaviors. Then if you're ready, write another goal to work on. Look back on page 74 to review how to write a goal.

If you're struggling, try to identify your obstacles. Then you can work on ways to overcome them. If needed, rewrite your goal to reflect your current desires and ability.

Remember, you are making changes that are meant to last a lifetime. Be patient, and keep up the good work.

Taking Charge of Your Diabetes

You know that you need to care for your diabetes every day. You are your own primary care giver. The more you know and understand about diabetes, the better you'll be able to manage it.

You've already learned a lot about diabetes and how to stay healthy. As time goes on, you will continue to learn and to increase your self-care skills.

Be sure to learn about the many opportunities for continuing diabetes education and support in your community. Your provider can help you identify classes, books, support groups, and other resources. Also, resources are listed on pages 115–116 of this book.

Remember, too, that your family and friends can be your strongest support system. Include them in your learning process. Share your experience of living with diabetes with them.

You are in control. Here's to your good health!

Congratulations!

This is to certify that

_____

Name

Completed the program

Insulin

BASICS

_____   _____

Educator   Date

APPENDIX

Diabetes Pills

Some of these medications are approved for use with insulin and may be recommended by your provider. The Food and Drug Administration approves new medications and formulations on an ongoing basis. Ask your provider for the latest information.

SULFONYLUREAS (SULFA-BASED). Stimulate the pancreas to release more insulin.

Generic Name (Trade Name)	Common Starting Dose	Maximum Daily Dose	Schedule for Taking
Glyburide (DiaBeta®)	1.25–5 mg	20 mg	1–2 times daily with meals
Glyburide (Micronase®)	1.25–5 mg	20 mg	1–2 times daily with meals
Glyburide (Glynase®)	1.50–3 mg	12 mg	1–2 times daily with meals
Glipizide (Glucotrol®)	5 mg	40 mg	1–2 times daily, 30 minutes before meals
Glipizide extended release (Glucotrol XL™)	2.5–5 mg	20 mg	1 time daily with meal
Glimepiride (Amaryl®)	1–2 mg	8 mg	1 time daily with meal

BIGUANIDES. Decrease the release of glucose by the liver and make the cells more sensitive to insulin.

Generic Name (Trade Name)	Common Starting Dose	Maximum Daily Dose	Schedule for Taking
Metformin (Glucophage®)	500–1000 mg	2550 mg	1–3 times daily with meals
Metformin extended release (Glucophage®XR)	500 mg	2000 mg	1 time daily with evening meal

THIAZOLIDINEDIONES. Make the cells more sensitive to insulin and decrease the release of glucose by the liver.

Generic Name (Trade Name)	Common Starting Dose	Maximum Daily Dose	Schedule for Taking
Pioglitazone (Actos®)	15-30 mg	45 mg	1 time daily
Rosiglitazone (Avandia®)	4 mg	8 mg	1-2 times daily

MEGLITINIDES. Stimulate the pancreas to release insulin over a shorter period of time (after meals).

Generic Name (Trade Name)	Common Starting Dose	Maximum Daily Dose	Schedule for Taking
Repaglinide (Prandin®)	0.5-1 mg	16 mg	2-4 times daily with meals
Nateglinide (Starlix®)	120 mg	480 mg	2-4 times daily with meals

ALPHA GLUCOSIDASE INHIBITORS. Slow the body's absorption of carbohydrates.

Generic Name (Trade Name)	Common Starting Dose	Maximum Daily Dose	Schedule for Taking
Acarbose (Precose®)	25 mg	300 mg	3 times daily with meals
Miglitol (Glyset®)	25 mg	300 mg	3 times daily with meals

COMBINATION PILLS. Two or more medications with complimentary actions combined in one pill.

Generic Name (Trade Name)	Common Starting Dose	Maximum Daily Dose	Schedule for Taking
Metformin/Glyburide (Glucovance®)	2.5 mg/ 500 mg	20 mg/ 2000 mg	1-2 times daily with meals

OTHER

Generic Name (Trade Name)	Common Starting Dose	Maximum Daily Dose	Schedule for Taking

Insulin BASICS Supply List

Your healthcare provider will help you fill out this list.

Blood glucose meter _____

Blood glucose test strips _____

Lancets _____

Insulin _____

Syringes _____

Ketone test strips _____

Sharps container _____

Glucagon kit _____

Medical identification _____

Other _____

Carbohydrate Adjustments for Physical Activity

These guidelines are a good place to start. But test your blood glucose levels before and after physical activity. Look at the results. This is the best way to find the correct carbohydrate adjustments for you.

Duration and Intensity of Physical Activity	Blood Glucose Level Before Physical Activity (mg/dL)		
	Less than 100	100–180	180–250
Short duration, low intensity Examples: 30-minutes of yoga, walking, or bicycling leisurely	Add 15 grams of carbohydrate	No adjustment needed	No adjustment needed
Moderate duration, moderate intensity Examples: 30–60 minutes of walking vigorously, playing tennis, swimming, or jogging	Add 15 grams of carbohydrate	Add 15 grams of carbohydrate for a blood glucose level of 100–120 No adjustment needed for blood glucose level of 121–180	No adjustment needed
Moderate duration, high intensity Examples: 30–60 minutes of running, aerobics, spinning, or kick boxing	Add 30 grams of carbohydrate	Add 15 grams of carbohydrate	No adjustment needed
Long duration, moderate intensity Examples: 1 hour or more of playing team sports, golfing, cycling, or swimming. (Retest your blood glucose level after each hour of activity, and add carbohydrate according to that blood glucose level.)	Add 15 grams of carbohydrate per hour of activity	Add 15 grams of carbohydrate per hour of activity	After the first hour of activity, add 15 grams of carbohydrate

Reprinted from Safe and Healthy Exercise for People with Diabetes, *©2001 International Diabetes Center, Minneapolis.*

Dining Out Favorites

If you count fat grams, women should aim for no more than 20–25 grams of fat per meal, and men should aim for no more than 25–35 grams. For side dishes or snacks, try to keep below 3 grams of fat per carbohydrate serving.

FAST FOOD	CARBOHYDRATE CHOICES
❤ Baked potato, plain (Wendy's)	5
Big Fish Sandwich® (Burger King)	4
Burger, large (Burger King Whopper®)	3
❤ Burger, small	2
Chicken breast, original (KFC)	1
Chicken burrito (Taco Bell)	3
Chicken McNuggets®, 6 (McDonald's)	1
❤ Chili, 12 ounces (Wendy's)	2
French fries, small	2
Onion rings, small	2½
Personal Pan Pizza®, pepperoni (Pizza Hut)	5
❤ Roast beef, regular (Arby's)	2
❤ Santa Fe Turkey Sandwich (Bruegger's)	4
❤ Turkey breast sandwich, 6" (Subway)	3

MEXICAN	
❤ Taco, 7" soft-shell	1
Beef enchilada, 6"	2
Burrito de frijole (bean), 9"	4
Chimichanga, 6 ounces	3
Nachos, with beef and beans, 6 to 8	3½
Taco salad, large	4
Taco, large, fried tortilla, sour cream	3
Quesadilla	2

❤ Smart choices for heart health or weight loss

INDIAN
- 💗 Chapati, 6" 1
- 💗 Naan, 1 small loaf 1
- 💗 Basmati rice, ½ cup 1
- Samosa, lamb-filled 1
- 💗 Dal (dhal), ½ cup 1

ASIAN
- 💗 Chicken and vegetables, 2 cups 2
- Egg roll, 1 small 1
- 💗 Chow mein, 2 cups 2
- Rice, fried, and meat, 1 cup 2
- Sweet and sour pork, 1½ cups 4
- 💗 Rice, white, 1 cup 3
- 💗 Wonton soup, 1 cup with 2 wontons 1

ITALIAN
- Cannelloni, 4 stuffed noodles 2
- 💗 Chicken cacciatore, ½ breast 1
- Fettuccini primavera, 1½ cups 2
- 💗 Lasagna, beef, 3" by 4" 1
- Manicotti, cheese with sauce, 2 3
- 💗 Marinara sauce, ½ cup 1

DESSERT AND SPECIALTY ITEMS
- Bismark (Dunkin Donuts) 3
- Blueberry muffin (Arby's) 2
- 💗 Cafe Latte, tall, nonfat milk (Starbucks) 1
- Cake, 2" square with frosting 2
- Cinnamon crisps (Taco Bell) 2
- Glazed Donut (Dunkin Donuts) 1½
- 💗 Honey-grain Bagel (Bruegger's) 4
- Sugar-free apple pie, ⅙ pie (Perkins) 4
- 💗 Sugar-free yogurt, ½ cup (TCBY) 1
- 💗 Vanilla cone, small (McDonald's) 1½

💗 Smart choices for heart health or weight loss

Physical Tune-up

You need to see your provider at least two to four times per year.

Check Points	Target	Initial Checkup Date:
Height		
Weight		
Blood Pressure	130/80 or less	
HbA$_{1c}$	Optimal: Less than 7% Desirable: Less than 7.5%	
Total Cholesterol	Optimal: less than 170 mg/dL Desirable: less than 200 mg/dL	
HDL	Optimal: 45 mg/dL or higher Desirable: 40 mg/dL or higher	
LDL	Optimal: Less than 100 mg/dL	
Triglycerides	Optimal: Less than 150 mg/dL Desirable: Less than 200 mg/dl	
EKG (electrocardiogram)	Normal	
Thyroid Function (TSH)	0.2–5.5 µIU/mL (may vary by lab)	
Urine Micro Albumin	less than 30 mg/G Cr	
Dental Exam		
Eye Exam (dilated pupil)		
Foot Exam		
Meter Check		

Target ranges for elderly may vary, so check with your provider.

3-Month Visit Date:	6-Month Visit Date:	9-Month Visit Date:	One-Year Visit Date:

Sample Menus

MENUS FOR WOMEN WHO WANT TO LOSE WEIGHT

Each menu has about 1,200 calories (2–3 carbohydrate choices per meal).

BREAKFAST

1 slice whole wheat toast
1 teaspoon margarine
⅓ melon
Coffee

BREAKFAST

Vegetable omelet (½ cup egg substitute, vegetables)
1 slice toast
1 teaspoon margarine
2 small plums

LUNCH

1 cup Chicken vegetable soup
½ sandwich (1 slice whole wheat bread, 2 ounces water-packed tuna, and 1 tablespoon fat-free or light salad dressing)
1 orange
Diet soft drink

LUNCH

1 cup spaghetti with ½ cup tomato sauce
Tossed salad with 2 tablespoons fat-free or light salad dressing
Coffee

DINNER

3 ounces grilled fish
1 small baked potato
1 cup broccoli
1 tablespoon low-fat sour cream
1 cup skim milk
1 cup strawberries

DINNER

1 low-calorie frozen dinner
1 cup green beans
1 cup skim milk

The menus on pages 110–113 are adapted from *Five Good Food Habits*, ©1995 by International Diabetes Center, Minneapolis.

MENUS FOR MEN WHO WANT TO LOSE WEIGHT OR WOMEN WHO WANT TO MAINTAIN WEIGHT

Each menu has about 1,500 calories (3–4 carbohydrate choices per meal).

BREAKFAST

1 English muffin

1 teaspoon margarine

½ cup orange juice

Sugar-free jam

Tea

LUNCH

Sandwich (2 slices bread, 1 ounce ham, 1 ounce low-fat cheese, mustard)

1 cup low-fat cabbage salad

1 apple

1 cup 1% milk

DINNER

1½ cups casserole (3 ounces turkey, pasta, vegetables, low-fat cream soup)

Tossed salad with 2 tablespoons fat-free or light salad dressing

Sugar-free gelatin

1 cup 1% or skim milk

BREAKFAST

1 cup oatmeal

1 cup 1% milk

Coffee

LUNCH

1 cup chili

6 saltine crackers

1 ounce low-fat cheese

Sugar-free gelatin

1 cup melon

Carrot and celery sticks

Sugar-free lemonade

DINNER

2 pieces vegetable pizza

1 piece fresh fruit

Diet soft drink

1 medium cookie

MENUS FOR MEN WHO WANT TO MAINTAIN WEIGHT

Each menu has about 1,800 calories (4–5 carbohydrate choices per meal).

BREAKFAST

2 pancakes (6" across)

1 egg

2 pieces toast

Sugar-free pancake syrup

1 teaspoon margarine

Coffee

LUNCH

Sandwich (2 slices bread, 2 ounces roast beef)

Green salad with 2 tablespoons fat-free or light salad dressing

1 apple

2 small low-fat cookies

1 cup skim milk

DINNER

2 cups chicken stir-fry (3 ounces of chicken, vegetables)

1 cup rice

1 fortune cookie

Tea

BREAKFAST

1½ cup dry cereal

1 cup 1% milk

2 tablespoons raisins

Tea

LUNCH

Large fast food hamburger (¼ pound with lettuce and tomato, no sauce)

Small fries

Diet soft drink

DINNER

4 ounces steak

1 medium baked potato with 1 tablespoon light sour cream

1 dinner roll with 1 tablespoon margarine

Tossed salad with 1 tablespoon fat-free or light salad dressing

1 cup mixed vegetables

1 cup low-fat milk

12–15 grapes

MENUS FOR ACTIVE MEN WHO WANT TO MAINTAIN WEIGHT

Each menu has about 2,400 calories (6–7 carbohydrate choices per meal).

BREAKFAST

1 large bagel

1 medium banana

2 teaspoons light cream cheese

BREAKFAST

1½ cups of Wheaties®

1 cup skim milk

½ cup juice

2 slices of toast

2 teaspoons margarine

LUNCH

12" club sandwich

1 ounce potato chips

Diet soft drink

LUNCH

1 turkey sandwich

1 bowl tomato soup

6 saltine crackers

Carrot and celery sticks

1 cup skim milk

1 medium cookie

DINNER

3 ounces round steak

1 cup new potatoes

1 slice Texas toast (2 ounces)

1 cup skim milk

½ cup light ice cream

DINNER

1½ cups of casserole

2 dinner rolls

1 green salad with low-fat dressing

1 diet soft drink

1 medium apple

HEALTHY SNACK IDEAS

Each choice contains about 15 grams of carbohydrate, 3 grams or less fat, and 250 mg or less sodium.

BREAD/CRACKERS

1 slice bread or toast
2 slices light bread
½ small bagel or English muffin
1 small low-fat muffin (1½ oz)
3 gingersnaps
3 graham cracker squares
4 Ry-Krisps®
5 reduced fat Triscuits®
5 vanilla wafers
6 saltines
6 SnackWells® Golden Crackers
8 animal crackers
12 Ritz Air Crisps®
15 reduced-fat Wheat Thins®
20 Cheese Nip Air Crisps®

FRUIT

1 medium piece of fresh fruit
1 small banana (or ½ large)
1 cup berries or melon
½ cup canned fruit (4 oz)
(in juice, water, or light syrup)
¼ cup dried fruit
12–15 grapes or cherries

SWEETS

½ cup Jell-O® (not sugar-free)
½ cup sugar-free pudding
1 frozen fruit bar
1 fudgsicle
⅓ cup frozen yogurt
6–8 oz artificially sweetened yogurt
½ cup low-fat ice cream
1 Rice Krispie® Treat (0.78 oz bar)
1 low-fat granola bar
2 small fat-free cookies
3 round hard candies

SNACK FOODS

10 Baked Lays® Potato Chips
10 Baked Tostitoes® Corn Chips
15 Old Dutch® Tiny Pretzel Twists
3 cups microwave popcorn, light
(JollyTime® Light or Smartpop®)
¾ cup dry, unsweetened cereal

BEVERAGES

1 cup fat-free milk
½ cup fruit juice
1 packet Swiss Miss® Lite Cocoa

OTHER

_____
_____
_____
_____
_____

Learning Resources

BOOKS FROM THE INTERNATIONAL DIABETES CENTER

Call (888) 637-2675 or order online at www.idcpublishing.com.

Convenience Food Facts by Arlene Monk RD, LD, CDE; and
Nancy Cooper, RD, LD, CDE

Arranged for ease of comparison-shopping, *Convenience Food Facts*
guides readers to low-fat choices among more than 3,000 popular brand-
name products. In addition, the book lists exchange values and carbohydrate choices—information not found on food labels.

The Convenience Foods Cookbook by Nancy Cooper, RD, LD, CDE

Turn brand-name foods into brand-new meals! Recipes in *The Convenience Foods Cookbook* transform packaged goods into healthy dishes.
Go from package to plate in less than 20 minutes!

Exchanges for All Occasions by Marion J. Franz, MS, RD, LD, CDE

Completely updated and reorganized, *Exchanges for All Occasions*
offers sample menus and comprehensive food lists that demonstrate how
you can include a variety of foods in a healthy diet. With this book as
your guide, you can enjoy all your favorite foods and stay healthy. Also
available in a pocket edition.

Fast Food Facts by Marion J. Franz, MS, RD, CDE

As a definitive guide to survival in the fast-food jungle, *Fast Food
Facts* shows you how to make wise selections at the top 40 fast food
chains. Includes meal exchanges, 'smart meals' and carbohydrate choices.
Also available in a pocket edition.

Managing Type 2 Diabetes by Arlene Monk RD, LD, CDE; Jan Pearson,
BAN, RN, CDE; Priscilla Hollander, MD, PhD; and Richard Bergenstal, MD

Managing Type 2 Diabetes is the perfect follow-up to Insulin
BASICS for people with type 2 diabetes. It is a comprehensive guide to
self-care and health care for type 2 diabetes. It includes all the information and tools you need to take charge of your health. Complete with
simple tables and charts to guide daily decisions, this easy-to-use book
addresses your concerns, answers your questions, and helps you live well
with diabetes.

HEALTHCARE RESOURCES

American Association of Diabetes Educators 100 West Monroe, Suite 400, Chicago, IL 60603, (800) 338-3633, www.aadenet.org

American Board of Podiatric Surgery 3330 Mission Street, San Francisco, CA 94110-5009, (415) 826-3200, www.abps.org

American Diabetes Association 1701 North Beauregard Street, Alexandria, VA 22311, (800) 342-2383, www.diabetes.org

The American Dietetic Association 216 West Jackson Boulevard, Suite 800, Chicago, IL 60606, (800) 366-1655, www.eatright.org

Canadian Diabetes Association 15 Toronto Street, Suite 800, Toronto, ON M5C 2E3, Canada, (800) 226-8164, www.diabetes.ca

Impotence World Association 119 South Ruth Street, Maryville, TN 37803, (800) 669-1603, www.impotenceworld.org

International Diabetes Center Affiliate Network 3800 Park Nicollet Boulevard, Minneapolis, MN 55416-2699, (888) 825-6315, www.idcdiabetes.org

National Eye Care Project PO Box 7424, San Francisco, CA 94120-7424, (800) 222-3937, www.eyenet.org

MEDICAL IDENTIFICATION

Medic Alert 2323 Colorado Avenue, Turlock, CA 95382, (888) 633-4298, www.medicalert.org

Monroe Specialty Company PO Box 740, Monroe, WI 53566, (608) 328-8381

MAGAZINES

Diabetes Forecast, American Diabetes Association, 1701 North Beauregard Street, Alexandria, VA 22314, www.diabetes.org/diabetesforecast

Diabetes Self-Management, 150 West 22nd Street, New York, NY 10011, (800) 234-0923, www.diabetes-self-mgmt.com

INTERNET RESOURCES

www.diabetesnet.com Offers general information about diabetes.

www.idcdiabetes.org Lists education programs for people with diabetes, their family members, and healthcare professionals, along with International Diabetes Center Affiliate Network sites in the United States.

www.idcpublishing.com E-commerce site offering publications developed by International Diabetes Center experts for people with diabetes, their family members, and healthcare professionals.

www.niddk.nih.gov National Institutes of Diabetes and Digestive and Kidney Diseases (National Institutes of Health)

SOFTWARE APPLICATIONS

Camit Roche Diagnostics, (800) 858-8072, www.roche.com/diagnostics/

In Touch LifeScan, Inc., 1000 Gibraltar, Milpitas, CA 95035, (800) 227-8862, www.lifescan.com

Mellitus Manager Metamedix, Inc., 735 East Ohio Ave., Suite 202, Escondido, CA 92025, or download a free copy of Mellitus Manager at www.metamedix.com

PrecisionQID Abbott/Medisense, Abbott Laboratories, Medisense Product Line, 4A Crosby Drive, Bedford, MA 01730-1402, (800) 527-3339, www.abbott.com

Win Glucofacts Bayer Corporation-Diagnostics, 511 Benedict Avenue, Tarrytown, NY 10591, (800) 255-3232, www.bayerdiag.com

Glossary

Blood Glucose Level The amount of glucose in the blood measured by a laboratory or self-test.

Carbohydrate Nutrient in foods such as starches, fruit, milk, and sweets. Carbohydrate is broken down into glucose for energy.

Carbohydrate Choice A measure used in carbohydrate counting. One carbohydrate choice is equal to 15 grams of carbohydrate.

Carbohydrate Counting A food planning method based on eating a set amount of carbohydrate at each meal and snack.

Cholesterol A fat-like substance that is found in food and made by the body. High total cholesterol is a risk for heart disease.

Total cholesterol includes HDL cholesterol (high-density lipoprotein), LDL cholesterol (low-density lipoprotein), and triglycerides. A high level of LDL increases the risk of heart disease. It is often called "bad" cholesterol. HDL is the "good" cholesterol. It carries LDL and triglycerides out of the blood and protects against heart disease. It's good to have high levels of HDL.

Exercise and weight loss help increase HDL levels. Eating a healthy, low-fat diet helps lower LDL levels.

Food Plan An individualized schedule of meals and snacks created to help a person with diabetes maintain a target blood glucose level and good nutrition.

Glucose A sugar made in the body when food is digested. It is the body's main source of energy.

Hemoglobin A_{1c} (HbA$_{1c}$) A blood test that shows the average blood glucose level over the last two to three months. It is used to evaluate diabetes control and to determine whether changes need to be made in a person's diabetes treatment plan.

Hyperglycemia A condition that occurs when the blood glucose level is higher than the target range.

Hypoglycemia A condition that occurs when the blood glucose drops lower than the target range.

Impaired Fasting Glucose or **Impaired Glucose Tolerance** Conditions in which a person's plasma blood glucose level is higher than normal but not high enough to be diagnosed as diabetes. Both conditions signal that the person is at risk for developing diabetes.

Insulin A hormone produced in the pancreas that allows glucose to get into cells. Without it, glucose cannot be used for energy.

Insulin-to-carboydrate ratio The number of units of bolus insulin that a person takes for each carbohydrate choice (15 grams) in their food plan.

Ketones A potentially harmful waste product created when the body breaks down fat for energy.

Meter A small machine used to measure the level of glucose in blood.

Pancreas A gland located near the stomach that makes insulin.

Test Strips Chemically treated paper or plastic strips used for a self-test of blood glucose levels.

Triglycerides Fats that are found in food and made by the body. High triglyceride levels increase the risk for heart disease.